OW

The Philosophy of Risk

John C. Chicken and Tamar Posner

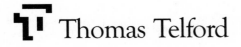 Thomas Telford

Published by Thomas Telford Publishing, Thomas Telford Services Ltd, 1 Heron Quay, London E14 4JD.
URL: http://www.t-telford.co.uk

Distibutors for Thomas Telford books are
USA: ASCE Press, 1801 Alexander Bell Drive, Reston, VA 20191-4400
Japan: Maruzen Co. Ltd, Book Department, 3–10 Nihonbashi 2-chome, Chuo-ku, Tokyo 103
Australia: DA Books and Journals, 648 Whitehorse Road, Mitcham 3132, Victoria

A catalogue record for this book is available from the British Library

ISBN: 0 7277 2666 8

Typeset by the Midlands Book Typesetting Company.
Printed and bound in Great Britain by Bookcraft (Bath) Limited.

Contents

1

Introduction

No lesson seems to be so deeply inculcated by the experience of life as that you never should trust experts. If you believe the doctors, nothing is wholesome: if you believe the theologians, nothing is innocent: if you believe the soldiers, nothing is safe.
Lord Salisbury (1830–1903)
British Prime Minister
1885–6, 1886–92 and 1895–1902.

An element of risk pervades all decision-making — from the simplest to the most complex decision — yet universally agreed rules for determining the acceptability of a risk are as elusive as the Holy Grail. The search for such rules is also complicated by the enormous range of views that exist on risk acceptability. The spectrum of perception of risk ranges from the qualitative views of the non-specialist to the views of the specialist who, with extensive data on the subject, is able to give a precise quantitative assessment of the risk.[1]

A recent review of research interests in risk in the social and economic area in academic institutions in the United Kingdom identified 170 areas, the subjects of interest ranging from the impact of safety cases on railway risk acceptability to risk management procedures, responsibility and blame in the National Health Service.[2] Areas of study also included

- the effect of safety legislation in controlling risk
- risk assessment in local government decision-making
- assessing the risks of the changing employment contract
- risk, child protection and the media.

1

The range of departments interested in risk is also equally diverse, which emphasises the many different facets of risk. In addition to interest in business schools, there is interest in risk in geography, economics, computing, sociology, psychology, public health, environmental and engineering departments. In business alone, interests in risk, risk assessment and risk management are very diverse, and range from banks to insurance companies and from project sponsors to those concerned with health and safety. These four examples are not intended to define completely the range of business interests in risk but just to illustrate how wide the interest is.

Our aim in writing this book is to give decision-makers, and those close to decision-makers, a logical philosophy of risk that will help them to determine in a consistent defensible way what is an acceptable risk. The approach we adopted was to examine several activities and from this examination to identify the factors common to all determinations of risk acceptability, thereby to develop a hypothesis about the aspects of risk that are universally acceptable. In building up our view of the common factors, we try, as far as possible, to base our views on the quantitative evidence; in this way, we hope to illustrate more precisely the magnitude of the variability and uncertainty associated with the argument and to avoid speciousness in our hypothesis. This approach we somewhat pretentiously describe as building a philosophy of risk.

Philosophy of risk

Philosophy has been described as consisting of many branches, for each of which the central concern is with criteria.[3] Although we argue that risk is a universal concept, inherent in every aspect of life, each activity has its own portfolio of characteristics. We have not attempted to consider every type of risk but have derived our conclusions from what we consider to be a representative sample of activities. The sample consists of risks associated with manufacturing, finance, major projects, transport and sport. In some cases the acceptability of risks has to be determined by considering the activity involved in isolation; more often, however, a combination of factors has to be considered.[4-7] Each type of risk is measured by its own unique set of dimensions, which may include the probability of death, the probability of losing money, the probability of a structure failing, net benefit and the probability of public opinion being against the activity in question.

Naturally occurring and man-made risks

Consideration also needs to be given to the fact that some risks can be categorised as natural catastrophes and others as man-made disasters. Natural catastrophes represent an important category of risk that we all have to accept. Between 1970 and 1988, natural and man-made disasters as measured by insured losses were at roughly the same level, but since 1988, natural disaster insured losses have been nearly three times higher than those of man-made disasters.[8] In the period 1970–1995, all but one of the 30 most costly insurance losses were due to natural events[9] and of the 20 worst catastrophes in 1995, 16 were due to natural disasters.[10] To help the reader understand the general nature of losses, additional data are given in Appendix 1.

It may be argued that some of the devastating consequences of natural disasters could be reduced if towns and industries were located away from rivers that are prone to flooding and from areas with a high risk of major earthquakes, and out of the path of severe storms. In many ways, the unpredictability of natural disasters characterises the uncertainty that has to be allowed for in all evaluations of the significance of risks. Natural disaster risks do not have a frequency or magnitude that can be forecast with precision; for example, it is suggested that global warming will lead to warmer, wetter, windier and more variable weather which will subject many buildings in Britain to conditions that they are not designed to withstand. It has been suggested that to meet these new extremes of weather, Britain's building codes should be revised to take account of the predicted changes in climate.[11] It is not clear just what the weather conditions are of which building codes should take account.

In this study, natural disasters are regarded as just one of the many risk factors that decision-makers have to consider in determining the acceptability of the risks associated with a particular proposal.

Weighting factors

Besides each risk being characterised by its own set of factors, it has to be recognised that the weighting of the importance of each factor varies from risk to risk. We hope that the relationships postulated between the array of factors and the acceptability of a risk will prove worthy of the name *risk philosophy* and prove to be a consistent aid in determining the acceptability of risks.

Currently, there is no formal aid to decision-making that fits every type of assessment of risk acceptability; this is particularly true of decisions

3

containing a significant element of socio-political risk.[12] It is recognised from the outset that the data that have to be used in such decision-making may be very *soft*, i.e. they are associated with a considerable degree of uncertainty. In our view, comprehensive risk assessment which is structured logically, and not based simply on intuition, gives decision-making a defensible logic. (The nature and role of comprehensive risk assessment is discussed further in chapter 9.)

Defending structured decision-making as logical involves four very sweeping assumptions.

(a)   The analyst involved has the appropriate skills and capabilities.
(b)   **All** the relevant factors are examined.
(c)   The weighting of the significance of each factor is established.
(d)   All the required data are available.

This is another way of saying that the soundness of any aid to decision-making depends on the quality of the analysis on which it is based, the appropriateness and accuracy of the data used, and the suitability of the criteria adopted for judging acceptability.

Inevitably, the construction of criteria for assessing risk acceptability involves several kinds of value judgement. The two essential characteristics of value judgements were very concisely described by Lord Ashby in the following way.[13]

> *Value judgements include a judgement about the confidence that can be placed on the data the judgement has to be based on.*
>
> *Anyone providing the means for achieving a particular end has the moral responsibility to question the acceptability of the means and the end.*

The discussion in the chapters that follow shows how the themes of confidence in data and moral responsibility are essential components of the argument that is developed.

How to use this book

The approach adopted in building up the justification for the philosophy of risk proposed is to divide the justification into nine chapters. In each chapter, a different aspect of the argument is examined. Chapter 2 deals with the essential features of philosophical analysis and concentrates on identifying the aspects of the analysis that will give decision-makers the most help in determining what is an acceptable risk.

The next six chapters are devoted to examining the nature and characteristics of the risks associated with six specific activities. Attention is focused not only on the risks currently accepted by those involved in the activities, but also on attempts to expose the aspects of risk associated with the activity that are common to all risk acceptability situations. We appreciate that this involves considerable extrapolation from a modest sample of activities to a very much wider world, but it is our belief that extrapolation is justified and helpful. In these chapters we try and illustrate risk acceptability with quantitative data on the risks associated with the six activities. This means that many tables of data have had to be included. Nevertheless, we believe that the tables will give the reader confidence in the arguments presented. Chapter 9 develops, from the findings in chapters 3 to 8, a form of risk acceptability assessment that is justifiable and transparent and can be applied to a wide range of situations.

Chapter 10, the last chapter of the book, distils the evidence and the arguments presented in the earlier chapters, and from the distillate a philosophy of risk acceptability has been developed that we hope will help the evaluation and determination of acceptable risks across a broad spectrum of activities.

It is hoped that the results of this study will give decision-makers a philosophy of risk acceptability that will help them determine in a consistent, defensible and transparent way the acceptability of the risks inherent in the decisions they have to make.

2

Essentials of philosophy

This chapter describes how the use of the term philosophy *is justified in this study. It also identifies what we consider to be the essential components of a philosophy of risk acceptability and how the components are associated with real decision-making.*

Components of a philosophy

The aim of this chapter is to present the essential features of philosophical argument that will assist the decision-maker to put risk into a perspective that will identify the decision likely to yield the most good for the greatest number. The term *most good* is used to suggest connotations of technical benefit and socio-political acceptability as well as economic value; we recognise that to suggest the concept of value in purely economic terms and to use this concept as the basis for identifying philosophy may conflict with some views on philosophy[14] although a degree of justification for such an approach is given by Schrader-Frechette.[15]

While philosophy takes many forms, it is used in this study to describe the accepted impact of all the practical factors that influence decisions about the acceptability of risk. It is our strict intention to avoid what Popper calls *scholasticism*, by which is meant a form of arguing without a serious problem.[16] Following the Popper line of analysis, the starting point for this study is the identification of the common sense or commonly accepted view of what is an acceptable risk; this view is critically examined in order to tease from it that which appears to withstand the test justifying its being called a philosophy. It is the ability of a proposition to withstand searching critical analysis that determines whether or not it justifies inclusion in the ranks of philosophies.

The essential feature of any test to determine the existence of a philosophy on a particular subject is to postulate a proposition and to determine how the evidence available satisfies it. The result of the test will show whether the proposition is acceptable, should be rejected, or should be modified. It must, however, be recognised that proof of acceptability of a proposition is only valid at the moment the proof is completed; situations change with time and what is valid at one moment may not be so seconds later. As the authors of this study we would be very happy if our analysis proves to be of lasting value!

A *definition of risk*

As pointed out earlier, there is no universally agreed set of rules applicable to evaluation of risk acceptability; this is hardly surprising when one considers that neither is there a single, agreed set of definitions of risk. For the purposes of this study risk is taken to mean the chance that harm will occur and our fundamental proposition is that

$$\textbf{Risk} = \textbf{Hazard} \times \textbf{Exposure}$$

A *hazard* is the way in which a thing or situation can cause harm, while *exposure* is the extent to which the likely recipient of the harm can be influenced by the hazard. It follows, that unless both hazard and exposure are present simultaneously there can be no risk.[17] To make sure that there is no misunderstanding about the way the term *risk* is used in the discussion that follows, the terms *harm* and *exposure* must be explained a little more. Harm is used as an all embracing term that covers injury, damage, loss of performance and financial loss. Exposure is intended to incorporate the concepts of frequency and probability.

The initial proposition

For this study the initial proposition is that any decision about risk acceptability involves a complex set of factors — shown in simplified form in Fig. 1. Before the overall significance of the factors can be determined, each must be carefully weighted according to its importance — a process which itself carries a risk of error that could invalidate the whole analysis. Each of the factors identified in Fig. 1 has many components,

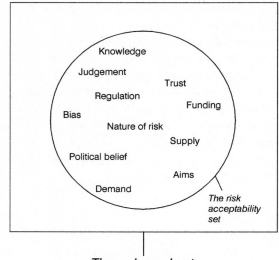

The universal set

Fig. 1. The risk acceptability set

an indication of which is given in Table 1. As the examination of the factors proceeds, it will become clear that the incorporation of a certain

Table 1. The general nature of each factor

Factor	General nature of each factor
Knowledge	Spectrum of known relevant information
Judgement	Critical assessment of the relevant knowledge
Trust	The extent to which each piece of information or a person involved is reliable
Regulation	The legal or official framework that constrains action that can be taken in various circumstances
Bias	The disposition to distort the significance of the various pieces of information that has to be used
Nature of risk	The magnitude and frequency of an unacceptable condition
Funding	The availability of the financial resources required to complete project/undertaking
Political belief	Compatability of project/undertaking/proposal with current sets of political beliefs
Aims	The objectives of groups/individuals/organisations involved with proposal. The aims are taken to include ethical and aesthetic considerations
Demand	The demand for the project/undertaking being proposed
Supply	The availability of alternative sources of supply

amount of numerical analysis of the evidence provides a sound logical foundation for the development of a philosophy. It must also be recognised, however, that some of the data that have to be used will be qualitative and subjective in origin; the problems associated with such data can be minimised by collecting and treating the data in a consistent manner. Only towards the end of the analysis is any attempt made to try to incorporate allowance for moral or political influences and in this way we attempt to avoid being relegated to what Russell defines as trivial philosophy.[18]

In the remainder of this chapter, each of the factors identified in Fig.1 and Table 1 is examined to determine their likely significance in the philosophy of risk; finally, the nature of the decision-making process is examined.

Knowledge

In the simplest sense, *knowledge* is the sum of what is known — either theoretically or in practice. At any one time a person's stock of knowledge is finite, but among this finite stock of knowledge, tools exist that will enable a person to refine their knowledge — either by deduction or induction. It is the fact that there are very great differences in the distribution of knowledge throughout the population that leads to the parties involved having differing views about what is acceptable, and gives rise to misunderstandings about the significance of risks; for these reasons, the process of establishing what is acceptable becomes very difficult. Those with little knowledge may be suspicious of the motives of proposers, and may consequently distrust and resist any proposals put forward by those with greater knowledge; by contrast, those with greater knowledge may have too much confidence in the adequacy of their knowledge and may inadvertently create greater risks than they intend.

Judgement

In this definition of the characteristics of components of factors in the risk acceptability set, judgement is not simply the final decision but is an integral part of the whole decision-making process. While the essential nature of judgement is the ability to make a critical assessment of evidence, there are important aspects of judgement that must also be considered. For example, judgements may be wrong — either because the evidence is wrong or incomplete, or because the assessment of the evidence is in error; judgements may also be biased — because the methodology is biased or because the judge is biased.

9

Sometimes a decision has to be based on subjective opinions which, by their very nature, are little more than informed guesses; decisions based on such opinions can only be regarded as indicative judgements and will have much larger margins of error associated with them than will judgements based soundly on hard, relevant, quantitative data.

Other components of the risk acceptability set — such as the constraints imposed by regulation or the economic factors which have a bearing on the availability of funding — may also influence judgements. Even the rules constraining the decision-making process — which may include cost/benefit principles, perceptual processes and production systems (the name given to the process of comparing alternatives) — could, it has been argued, have the effect of producing biased judgements.[19]

Trust

For there to be any progress towards solving a problem between two or more people, there must be a considerable degree of trust between the parties involved. If one party cannot trust the information that the other party presents, progress will at best be slow and if something one party presents is found to be false, trust between the parties will be destroyed and much time and effort will be required to restore that trust.[20]

An important prerequisite is that the parties involved understand in detail the issue that is being considered and that communication between the parties is open and in a form that may be understood by all involved. This, in turn, means that there should be no distortions which would tend to obscure the meaning, significance and implications of the information presented.

In any new situation the parties involved will, until trust is established, treat anything presented by the other parties with a considerable degree of scepticism; only as confidence in the correctness of the information is built up will trust begin to develop.

Regulation

Regulation interacts with risk philosophy in two important ways: the first is the influence of the philosophy on the way current regulations define the acceptability of risk; the second is the fact that the philosophy may change, leading to a demand for a particular regulation to limit more strictly the risk. These two aspects of regulation illustrate that the philosophy of risk acceptability may have different meanings at different times — aspects which are explored in more detail later in this book.

In a way the argument is about which comes first, the philosophy or the regulation? In an ideal world, the philosophy would come first but, in practice, the two may often develop in parallel. This has many disadvantages, not least of which is the fact that development in parallel or with regulation lagging behind tends to slow down the decision-making process because of dissatisfaction with the level of risk protection provided by the developing regulations compared to current risk acceptability.

Bias

Reference has already been made to the fact that distortion or bias in information can destroy trust between parties trying to solve a problem or to reach an agreement. Bias in discussion or information is not necessarily introduced with the intention of persuading people to a particular point of view; it may enter into data unintentionally — for example, through careless collection of data, as a result of weaknesses in the sampling system or analytical methodology, or perhaps because the subject being studied is not fully understood. It may even be that whole areas of the spectrum of data required have been missed out through ignorance or convention. There are some bureaucratic systems of decision-making that have been developed by excluding certain factors from the process; decisions based on such systems will at best be doubtful.

Alertness to the possibilities of bias requires all parties to have a sceptical view of the validity of information presented until the information has been proved to be trustworthy. Bias and trust in many ways colour many business dealings and decision-making in general.

Nature of risk

There is an element of risk in practically every aspect of life; it follows that risk takes many forms and it is a fact that most major decisions will involve several forms of risk.

Perhaps the simplest way to summarise the nature of risk is to say that it is a measure of the uncertainty about the ultimate consequences of a particular activity. Therefore, any precise discussion of the acceptability of a risk must describe the risk in quantitative terms; if the risk is described only in soft, qualitative terms, any conclusions about its acceptability will be equally soft or, to put it another way, will be merely uncertain speculation. In the chapters that follow, the risks associated with several aspects of life are examined in an effort to identify what, if any, characteristics the risks have in common.

Funding

Virtually everything in life has to be paid for in some way; every project — be it the purchase of a new shirt, a new refrigerator, even the next meal — has a price ticket on it. For major projects such as the development of a new aircraft or a new drug, the price is extremely high, but for all projects — humble or grand — there are options; at the very least there is generally the option of whether or not to go ahead.

It is often possible to derive a rating of the acceptability of the various options by comparing the benefits that would be obtained by spending the available funds in different ways; the risk can then be described in terms of the chance that, by spending the funds in a certain way, the result will fail to achieve maximum satisfaction. However, if a project is judged simply in terms of the amount of money involved, some very deep philosophical problems are posed and there is a distinct possibility that the units in which the benefits are described will not give a sufficiently comprehensive indication of their significance.

Political belief

Political beliefs may be very important in determining how funds are allocated to projects and what spectrum of projects should be funded. For example, one political belief could be that the majority of the funds available should be allocated to improving health services and education; an alternative political belief may dictate that all available funds should be shared between expenditure on defence, education, the environment and transport. With this very simple illustration, it may be seen that when projects depend on government funding, changes in government policy can affect the availability of funding. In a similar manner, changes in company policy or ownership can change the pattern of funding available for company projects. In other words, political beliefs can influence the priority allocated to projects aimed at keeping risks below a particular level.

Aims

To a large extent, the aims of an organisation will determine the types of thing to which its resources are directed. A car maker may want to

12

develop a new model, a food manufacturer may want to develop a new food product, an insurance company may want to market a new type of policy and a store may want to start selling a new range of goods.

Aims are rarely constant but change with time; this may mean that some risk-reducing proposals fall outside the aims of an organisation and require those aims to be modified before the proposal can be undertaken. It is also possible that, during the life of an organisation, its aims may be changed in ways that eliminate some risks or introduce new or unknown risks.

Demand

Demand could be seen as the driving force for all activities. If there is no demand for a product, no matter what form it takes, there can be no justification for producing it. A product that has been made with no use in sight and that ends up in storage is a waste of the resources that have gone into its production and a waste of the resources used in its storage. Similarly, products manufactured to specifications that do not align with customer demand — e.g. a product life of three months when customer demand is for a ten-year product life represent inefficient use of resources.

It should be assumed that the demands that have to be met are ethical demands, i.e. they are morally right and acceptable. While we must accept that the real world is far from ideal, we should nevertheless be working towards the ideal.

Supply

If there are several competing suppliers, there will be a risk that a price war could lower the price for which a particular project could be undertaken. In an extremely competitive supply situation, suppliers with no alternative product to fall back on may go bankrupt; this is a risk that has to be considered. It is also possible, however, that a lower price may increase demand, or that an organisation will be able to undercut its competitors and increase its market share.

Taken together, the factors of supply and demand define the market for particular goods or activities. Variations in supply and demand — in particular, variations that are likely to occur over time — represent risks that the decision-maker has to evaluate; therefore, criteria for judging their acceptability are required.

13

Nature of the decision-making process

Decision-making takes many forms and it is therefore difficult to undertake a comprehensive, uniform and consistent evaluation. This section endeavours to clarify decision-making by describing and categorising the main types of decision and discussing the nature of the problems associated with each category.

Decision-making can be described in such deceptively simple terms as *agreeing the course of action required* but simple definitions may well obscure many of the important nuances associated with the various parts of the decision-making process.

The first step towards identifying the type of decision required is to identify the essential elements of the environment surrounding the process. The decision-making environment is just one part of the universal environment which includes all real and transcendental systems. The elements of the real systems set most relevant to the decision-making process are shown in Fig. 2. One variable the figure does not show is time. This is because the influence of time is ubiquitous, influencing impartially both the explained and the explanatory variable in the argument; time, therefore, has to be allowed for in the assessment of each variable.

Each of the elements identified represents a complete group of relevant factors so that taken together the elements define all the factors that make up the environment surrounding the decision-making process. It

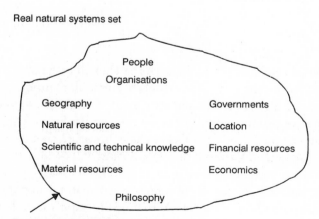

Fig. 2. Elements of the real systems set relevant to the decision-making process set

is not intended to imply that the factors are independent; in most cases there is interaction between them that tends to modify their significance and role. The significance of any factor may also additionally vary with time, for example, at the conceptual stage of a major project the importance of funding is low but at the construction and implementation stages the demand for funding is real and can be very significant even in national terms.

Table 2 illustrates some of the ways that the environment surrounding a decision may change with time. It is emphasised that with the passage of time the need for a decision may either increase or decrease, reflecting changes in demand.

The need for a decision can, with some justification, be described as being generated by various elements in the environment surrounding the decision-making process. For the purposes of this study the decision-making process is defined as

> the interaction between elements within the decision-making set that result in determination of how demands that arise can be most acceptably satisfied with the resources available.

This concept of decision-making as an interaction between the related elements of a set is illustrated in Fig. 3 which shows the decision-making process as a continuum from the emergence to the fulfilment of the demand. The nature of the interactions is different at each stage, but there is generally a peak in their intensity some time before completion of the main nodes in the process. In the case illustrated, it was assumed that the action necessary to implement the decision was taken. However, it is also recognised that in some cases the decision may be to take no action; in such cases the continuum would end at the T_2 — the point when the preliminary decision is made. Moreover, in a real environment

Table 2. Examples of changes possible with time in the decision-making environment

Decision variable	Changes that may occur with the passage of time
Knowledge	Improved knowledge may show proposal no longer appropriate or must be modified
Resource requirement	Demand for resources in terms of material, finance or manpower may be different to that originally predicted
Requirement for decision	Demand for decision and action may increase or decrease

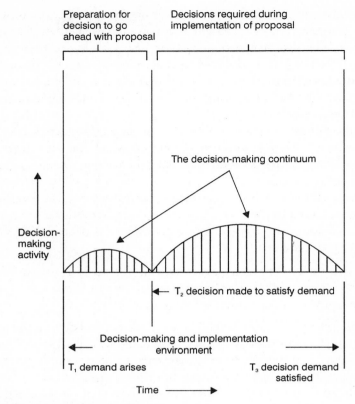

Fig. 3. Decision-making continuum

there may be several, interdependent major decisions which, taken together, constitute a formal decision-making procedure.

The significance of the variables — even the philosophy of what is an acceptable risk — may change over the life of the decision-making process, reflecting changes with time in demands and aspirations; where scientific or technological developments are involved, the changes that may have to be allowed for in the decision can be quite dramatic.

In the real world, decisions range from the small — involving only insignificant demands on resources — to the large, where the commitment of nationally significant quantities of resources may be involved. A small decision could be determining how many bolts to order, while a large decision could be deciding whether or not to order a new power station. Between these two extremes there is a whole spectrum of decision sizes but neither size nor importance gives a complete description of a decision; the important parameter, the parameter that has to be evaluated in assessing the implications of all decision options, is the associated risk or uncertainty.

An alternative way of categorising decisions is according to purpose; this may be domestic, internal to an organisation, external — nationally or internationally — to an organisation, regulatory in the national or the international sense. Complex decisions which involve consideration of the whole matrix of technical, economic and socio-political factors are termed comprehensive decisions; simple decisions, by contrast, will involve consideration of only parts of the matrix.

Tables 3 and 4 attempt to classify the various types of decision. The classification is somewhat arbitrary but it serves to illustrate the range of decision-making situations considered. Table 3 concerns the nature of simple decisions and Table 4 the general nature of comprehensive decisions.

As has already been stated, comprehensive decisions involve consideration of the technical, economic and socio-political groups of factors, and it was in order to deal with such disparate factors that the risk ranking technique was devised. The adequacy of the risk

Table 3. The nature of simple decisions

Scope of decision	Size of decision		
	Small	Medium	Large
Organisational	Deciding how to design a small component of secondary significance	Deciding which machine to buy	Deciding to extend production facilities
National	Deciding to adopt a new technical standard	Deciding which design to adopt for a nationally marketed product	Deciding the level for a major nationally marketed commodity
International	Deciding to adopt an international system of units	Deciding to join and participate in an international research project	Deciding that an organisation should operate in several countries
Regulatory	Deciding which factories to inspect	Deciding the level of contamination that must not be exceeded	Deciding a specific plant must be subject to detailed assessment before it can be allowed to operate

Table 4. The general nature of comprehensive decisions

Scope of decision	Size of decision		
	Small	Medium	Large
Organisational	A decision by a committee to accept a research project	A decision by trade unions and management to agree on modifications to work patterns in a particular company	A decision by a large national company to change its product range
National	A decision by a government committee to accept comment on a discussion document	A decision between management and trade unions in a particular industry to accept a new wage structure for the industry	A decision by Parliament to pass new legislation
International	A decision by an international body to accept a particular subject for investigation	A decision by an international organisation to allocate a large part of its budget to support a project in one country	A decision to build a fixed transport link between England and France across the English Channel
Regulatory	A decision about whether a transgression of a particular rule should be taken to court	Decision about the introduction of new rules on the maximum radiation levels allowable	A decision about the acceptability of a site for a major new process plant

ranking technique for providing an easily understood, clear and comprehensive evaluation of the evidence and giving the decision-maker a coherent, consistent and logical means of assessing the merits of various options is examined in later chapters, particularly chapters 9 and 10.

The conclusions about decision-making that appear to be warranted and that influence the nature of risk acceptance philosophy are, therefore, that

● there is a very large range of size and complexity of decision-making situations

- the problem of defining the basis of a decision and the weight given to the various factors involved is central to any explanation of a decision
- it may not be possible to explain the significance of every factor to the same degree of accuracy — particularly when novel features are involved.

In the chapters that follow the risks associated with manufacturing industry, the financial sector, major projects, medical risks, transport risks and risks in sport are examined. From this examination an attempt is made to identify a justifiable philosophy for determining what is an acceptable risk in various circumstances.

3

Risks in the manufacturing industry

The view of manufacturing industry taken in this chapter is very broad, embracing all processes that produce some tangible, physical product. Equally wide is the range of risks considered which cover changes in demand to changes in production technology.

The aims of this chapter are to identify the risks associated with the manufacturing industry in general and to develop a methodology for assessing the acceptability of such risks. The chapter is divided into three parts

- (a) the spectrum of risks associated with manufacturing industry
- (b) how the risks can be assessed
- (c) the optimum methodology for assessing the acceptability of manufacturing risks.

Spectrum of risks associated with manufacturing industry

Broadly, there are two categories of risk associated with manufacturing industry — external and internal risk. Some of the more obvious external and internal risks are identified in Tables 5 and 6. These risks could be described as changes in demand and changes in capability to satisfy the customer but all the risks — of whatever type — have serious financial implications for both the supplier and the customer. As will be seen in the next section, this means that all the parties involved have to make assessments of the risks to which they are exposed.

As shown in Table 6, internal risks take many forms. Some of these forms could be described as being related to quality control and the fact

Table 5. Some external risks in manufacturing industry

Risk	Implications
Demand for project changes	Changes to production have to be made on a timescale that satisfies customer
Competitors enter market at lower price	Either reduce price or lose market share
New technology replaces product	Either adapt product line to new technology or lose market
New regulations/standards require product to be changed	Either satisfy new regulations/standards or lose market share
Raw material supplies interrupted	Find alternative supply of raw materials or risk losing customer
Labour force goes on strike	Find some other way of getting product manufactured or risk losing customer
Cash flow problems mean suppliers and labour cannot be paid so they will not be available in the future	Either obtain finance or risk going out of business
War/terrorism/vandalism destroys or reduces production capacity	Find alternative means of production

Table 6. Some internal risks in the manufacturing industry

Risk	Implications
Machines or plant breaks down	Late delivery to customers leaves them dissatisfied and they change suppliers
Product made does not satisfy customer's requirements	Unacceptable product leaves customer dissatisfied and they change suppliers
Plant production cannot be changed quickly enough to satisfy customer's demands	Might result in loss of customer
New labour force cannot use machines efficiently	Requires new source of production to be found
Increase in labour costs means customer's requirements cannot be met at agreed price	Either negotiate new contract price, or find cheaper means of production or lose contract
Defect found with product months after it has been delivered to client	The cost of correcting defect has to be borne by supplier
Fire at factory interrupts deliveries to customer	Either find alternative way of supplying customer or risk losing customer

that in any product stream there are variations between different parts of the stream. These variations may be within accepted limits, but recognition of possible variation also implies recognition that the product may, on some occasions, be out of tolerance and unacceptable. No matter what form a product takes — be it a food product such as butter, pharmaceuticals, crankcases for motor car engines, pressure vessels for chemical plants or concrete for bridges — this argument is equally applicable. Table 7 lists some possible sources of variations and includes variations in raw materials, manufacturing processes, inspection procedures and even storage and transport. The list is not intended to be exhaustive but it does serve to illustrate the wide range of factors that need to be considered.

Most of the changes that take place in manufacturing have their origins in research. The transference of the results of research to a profitable application in manufacturing is itself associated with many risks, as illustrated in Table 8 which exemplifies the range of manufacturing/research transfers; the examples are drawn from projects with which the Steinbeis Foundation for Economic Promotion has been involved. (The Steinbeis Foundation is a unique organisation based in Germany which operates at 82 locations, with project and business partners in 51 countries:[21] in 1995 the organisation had a staff of 3716, a budget of 127 million Deutschmarks and completed 23 937 projects.)

Table 7. Some of the variations that may be associated with manufacturing processes

Aspect of manufacturing considered	Examples of variations
Raw materials	Raw materials may include unexpected impurities that may not be detected or allowed for in the manufacturing processes
Manufacturing processes	Manufacturing parameters may vary and produce a product that does not satisfy requirements. For example, pressure and temperature in a chemical process may vary and produce an unacceptable product. In an engineering factory worn machines may produce components with the wrong dimensions
Inspection procedures	Inspection procedures rarely cover 100% of the product and are generally based on a sampling procedure. Measurements are not absolute
Storage	Product may deteriorate in storage
Transport	Product may be damaged in the process of being transported from producer to user

Table 8. Examples of research transfers to manufacturing

Product	Research transfer
Plastic ball socket	Material with good sliding properties, resistant to harsh environments and does not require special tools for assembly
Colour printing — reduction in use of isopropanol	Improved method of measuring concentration of isopropanol
Automated control of paint spraying to give subject sprayed a uniform finish all over	Control system capable of learning shapes to be sprayed so that finish is of higher quality
Improvement to draught frame screen printing	Automatic screen tensioning and pattern setting and storage gives faster production
Insulated stainless steel waste gas system chimney	Chimney uses vacuum insulation instead of mineral wool. Guaranteed service life of ten years and vacuum guaranteed for whole of service life

Two types of risk are exposed by the examples given in Table 8.

(a) The proposed solution will fail and give a negative return on investment.

(b) The proposed solution will be successful and will sweep the market for the manufacturer; thus manufacturers who do not adopt this solution will lose business.

While research is often described as *blue sky*, i.e. designed to reveal the as yet unforeseen, it may nevertheless be very practical and concerned directly with the way manufacture is organised. A particularly interesting example of organisational change is demonstrated by the motor industry which, led by the Japanese motor manufacturers, cut their production and component costs by changing their relations with their suppliers. The process involved the development of a greater partnership between the component supplier and the main manufacturer, and required that the component supplier should be integrated into the whole process of developing new models and improving production efficiency and quality. American companies followed suit, an example being the Chrysler Company which reduced its suppliers from 2500 to 1140[22] and benefited to the extent that, since 1991, its pre-tax return on assets (percentage of assets) has been considerably greater than that of either Ford or General Motors. In risk terms this illustrates the financial penalty faced by a manufacturer that fails to keep its organisation up to the standards of the competition.

The risks considered so far are those that have obvious implications for the commercial viability of the organisations involved. No less significant, however, are the risks associated with the safety of people and plant, the health of the workforce, consumers and such members of the public as may be affected by the manufacturer's activities and, increasingly, the potential to cause damage to the environment. Table 9 shows the order of the fatal injury rate in some sectors of British manufacturing and it goes without saying that care must be taken to keep the risks of fatal injuries to a minimum.

Attention must be paid to possible causes of occupational ill health; in Britain about 2·2 million people suffer from ill health caused or made worse by their work, and millions of working days are lost as a result. The lost time is not distributed uniformly throughout the working population[23] (Table 10) and, although the working days may seem a small proportion of the total number of working days, it is not only the direct cost that has to be considered but also the likelihood that someone developing an illness due to their work will sue for compensation. In a recent case, an employee who claimed to have been overstressed by his work was awarded £175 000 damages by the court[24, 25] — a figure to which must be added the legal costs of defending the case and the indirect costs of the ensuing bad publicity. The financial argument is very powerful. The Health and Safety Executive estimates that accidents and work-related ill-health results in over 30 million working days lost at a cost to industry of almost £700 million.[26] The overall cost of work accidents and work-related ill health to employers is estimated to be between £4 billion and £9 billion a year. This is equal to between 5% and 10% of gross trading profits. The total cost to society as a whole is estimated at between £10 billion and £15 billion. This is equivalent to almost 3% of the country's gross domestic product. For the individual organisation, the value of reducing its losses due to injury and ill health is clear.

Table 9. The order of fatal injury rates in British manufacturing industry

Type	Individual risk ($\times 10^{-6}$, per year)
Professional and scientific services	1
Electrical engineering	6
Paper, printing and publishing	11
Chemicals and allied industries	19
Transport and communication	33
Metal manufacturing industry	76

Table 10. Summary of health risks associated with work

Health risk	Ill-health effects	Frequency
Handling heavy or awkward loads. Poor work postures; repetitive or forceful movements; a combination, e.g. repetitive assembly and inspection work.	Musculoskeletal disorders, e.g. bad backs; pains, strains and sprains; 'RSI'; upper limb disorders	About 5·4 million working days a year are lost in Britain due to this problem
Breathing in and handling hazardous substances, e.g. asbestos; solvents; isocyanates, wood, grain and silica dust; sheep dips; other chemicals	Cancer; asthma; bronchitis; fibrosis; poisoning; dermatitis; burns	About 1000 new cases a year in Britain
High noise levels, e.g. from noisy tools and machinery	Deafness; tinnitus	About 100 000 people in Britain are believed to have suffered hearing damage due to their work. About 80% of compensation claims are due to noise
Vibration, e.g. from hand-held tools; regularly driving vehicles	Vibration white finger with pain in fingers and loss of grip; low back pain from whole body vibration	
Exposure to radiations, e.g. from x-ray work; ultraviolet radiation from prolonged outdoor work; infra-red; lasers	Burns; skin complaints; eye damage; cancer	
Exposure to biological agents — viruses, bacteria, fungi and parasites — e.g. in health care, agricultural and laboratory work	Mild sickness to serious diseases, e.g. orf; hepatitis B; legionnaires' disease	
Stressors — e.g. excessive workload or work pace; conflicting priorities	Can contribute to high blood pressure; heart disease; depression	

The assessment of health risks associated with work is frequently made more difficult by the fact that the adverse results — noise-induced hearing loss is a case in point — are often not manifest until several years have elapsed. Such a delay also complicates the assessment of the risks that may lead gradually to environmental damage such as contamination of land or aquifers. What is accepted today as best practice for environmental protection may, in the future, turn out to have been in error. The consequences of pollution may not manifest themselves immediately and it may be years before the implications of the pollution are known. While it is generally accepted that the polluter pays, the law does not generally impose retrospective liability — The House of Lords verdict on *Cambridge Water Co.* v. *Eastern Counties Leather plc* (ECL) case.[27] ECL used organochlorines as solvents for degreasing leather as part of their tanning process. Owing to their method of handling the organochlorines up to 1976, some of the material escaped from the factory into the water flowing to a borehole 1·3 miles away. Contamination of the water drawn from the borehole by Cambridge Water Company was acceptable by the standards then in use. In 1980 the European Commission issued a directive that reduced the acceptable level of organochlorines in water to a tenth of the level previously accepted. Cambridge Water brought a case against ECL — at the Appeal level it was held that ECL were liable for damages of over £1 million. The case went to the House of Lords and they ruled, as mentioned above, that the law cannot impose retrospective liability. If people comply with the law as it currently exists they cannot be guilty of not satisfying stricter laws that are introduced sometime in the future. This case shows some of the aspects of the risk implications of changes in regulation.

It is evident from the above that manufacturing risks cover a very broad and complex field. What is interesting, however, is how the size of an enterprise introduces differences in the approach to management of risk.

The single owner, developing a small firm, will be concerned to stay in business and, if possible, to expand. Such a person will be acutely aware that demand for the original product may fall and lead to such a reduction in profits that the business must fail unless it can change to producing another profitable product. Falling demands and decreasing returns, characteristic of extractive and bulk production industries,[28] are not the only possibilities; the reverse — expanding demand and increasing returns — is also feasible, particularly in the knowledge-based industries. The owner of a small business will see changes in demand as one of the most critical risk factors that has to be kept under review; in larger organisations where there are more people involved, there is a tendency for the individual's sense of personal responsibility to be diminished and the view that someone else has responsibility for risks often becomes endemic.

All companies are likely to be concerned about a similar range of risk factors which, in addition to those already described, might include

- disruption of supplies of materials
- supply of defective materials
- breakdown of production machinery
- staff problems
- product proving to be defective which leads to many claims for compensation
- upward change in demand requiring an increase in production facilities.

However, larger companies, which will probably have a diversified range of products and greater resources to call on, are likely to have more options open to them for the way in which the risks may be dealt with.

All companies are also at some risk from predators wishing to buy them up. The small company, if the owner holds all or most of the shares, will be quite well able to resist — unless the predator has some other form of control such as a near monopolistic position in the supplies market; the situation for large companies can be much more complex.

How the risks can be assessed

The concerned entrepreneur needs helpful advice on the assessment of practical business risks. The approach which follows is based on soft system methodology — particularly the work of Checkland[29, 30] — with the aim not only of assessing each risk factor but also of considering their integrated impact by means of a five step analysis.

Step 1. Identify the set of factors that make up the business environment.

Step 2. Identify the factors that interact with one another to produce either a positive or a negative impact on the business environment.

Step 3. Assess the weighting that should be given to the importance of individual factors.

Step 4. Assess the overall impact of the various positive and negative factors.

Step 5. Assess what changes in the significance of the factors identified are likely to take place over the next 1, 5, 10, 15 and 20 years.

From the assessment of the changes predicted over the various time scenarios, determine what changes must be made to the company's plans for the future. The action taken will depend to a large extent on the entrepreneur's risk philosophy.

An important concern about using any analysis to attempt to predict the future is the degree of uncertainty that must be associated with the results of such analysis. The three main sources of uncertainty, which must be taken into account in any attempt to use the methodology, are

(a)   The analysis may not have identified/incorporated all the factors that influence the future.

(b)   The data used on each factor may be very imprecise and may be little more than guesses.

(c)   The whole portfolio of assumptions about future conditions and demand patterns may have been in error.

All this underlines why it is critical in the first step to identify the set of factors that has to be considered and why, in the second step, the interactions need to be identified; the process, in effect, amounts to building a model of the risk system involved.

The earlier part of this chapter listed six factors for consideration — a gross simplification of the number of factors that may in fact be needed. In practice, several hundred factors may initially have to be considered and, as the analysis proceeds, grouped together or eliminated. Table 11 provides a longer list of possible factors but even this only shows the range of factors that has to be kept in mind; a detailed risk assessment will have its own unique set of factors and it must always be remembered that there will be a degree of uncertainty associated with each one.

Having identified all the factors relevant to the case under consideration, the next step is to assign to each a weighting appropriate to its importance. If the situation is identical to one which has occurred in the past, it is possible that a body of quantitative evidence on appropriate weightings will exist. In reality, it is rarely the case that future situations replicate past situations exactly and new conditions that alter the pattern of weights often occur.

However tempting it may seem, a decision-maker cannot walk away from a situation; action must be taken and the challenge is to know what is likely to be the best decision. In Fig. 4 the basic steps in the process of decision-making are shown diagrammatically. An element of uncertainty about the significance of factors is associated with each step and the decision maker requires to know the limits of these uncertainties.

In a simplified way the range of uncertainty can be expressed as follows

Factor U_L = sum of factors that influence life of demand for product (these are essentially the internal factors)

$$= \Sigma \, U_T + U_{MAT} + U_{MAN} + U_U \qquad (3.1)$$

where U_T is the change in technology factor

Table 11. Some of the factors that have to be included in the assessment of the risk facing a manufacturing company

Product	Is demand increasing, falling or constant?
New demands	Product wanted in a different form — larger, smaller, faster, more accurate, cheaper, delivery phased to match clients requirements, product can be used in more hostile environments
Political factors	Wars in other parts of the world may cause changes in demand pattern and supply of raw materials
Economic factors	Exchange rate changes may reduce export markets. Changes in interest rates may make borrowing to finance future developments unattractive. Cash reserves may be too small to finance future developments. Market too small to allow company to operate at a profit
Factory equipment	Not adequate to meet future demands and has to be replaced, competitors have more efficient equipment
Human resources	Inadequate skilled human resources available to support development of company as required

U_{MAT} is the change in material factor
U_{MAN} is the change in manufacture factor
U_U is the change in use factor.

There will be a spectrum of estimates of U_L these will be a high, low and best estimate. Describing the best estimate as middle, average or central has been avoided.

The three values of U_L are identified as U_{LL}, U_{LB} and U_{LH}.

Similarly, with the U_E factor

The U_E = sum of factors that disturb the pattern of demand or production (these are essentially the external factors)

$$= \Sigma\, U_w + U_e + U_t \qquad (3.2)$$

where U_w is the change due to war or terrorism
U_e is the change due to economic environment
U_t is the change due to theft or fraud.

Like U_L there will be a spectrum of estimates of U_E, these will be a high, low and best estimate.

The three types of estimate U_E are identified as U_{EL}, U_{EB} and U_{EH}.

For most real projects the number of factors that have to be considered are greater than shown above.

$$\text{The total risk } U_{TOT} = U_L + U_E \qquad (3.3)$$

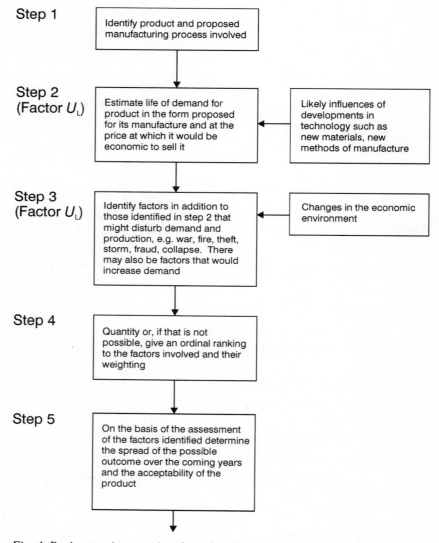

Fig. 4. Basic steps in assessing the risks inherent in manufacturing a particular product

The spectrum of values of U_L and U_E will mean that there will also be a spectrum of values of U_{TOT} from a bottom value U_{TOTL} to a top value U_{TOTH}. The factors considered in practice may be different to those included in equations (3.1), (3.2) and (3.3) as the factors considered have to be tailored to suit the specific nature of the proposition considered. The results of this type of analysis can take the form shown in Fig. 5.

So far only the operational features of decision-making have been considered and no allowance has been made for the aims and ambitions of the decision-maker — assuming the decision-maker is the owner of the enterprise under consideration, or has at least been given authority to act for the owner. The criteria by which an owner will judge accept-ability will generally be self-determined but if the decision-maker is an employee such criteria are likely to have been predetermined by someone else; this is an important difference between the ways in which owners and employed persons would make decisions.

Although there are many possible ways of categorising criteria for judging acceptability of risk, the two most important are commercial and political. Commercial criteria assume most relevance to organisa-tions which depend for their survival on making a profit while political criteria are important to enterprises which depend on government funding to support their activities. It must be appreciated that between the

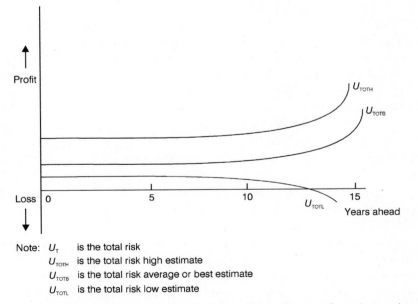

Note: U_T is the total risk
U_{TOTH} is the total risk high estimate
U_{TOTB} is the total risk average or best estimate
U_{TOTL} is the total risk low estimate

Fig. 5. Graphical representation of the risk analysis of a manufacturing project

primarily commercial and primarily political types of organisation there are many hybrid organisations that share both characteristics. Hybrid organisations would include, for example, state run industries, services provided by the state and firms dependent on government contracts.

For a commercial organisation the ultimate criterion will be that the proposed project makes a return on investment while ensuring that all relevant regulations and other constraints are satisfied. Where an organisation is primarily driven by political considerations, the main criterion will be that the project satisfies the role determined by the political masters and this may be quite remote from any consideration that can be measured in commercial terms.

Optimum methodology for assessing the acceptability of manufacturing risks

The structure of this assessment methodology is shown in Fig. 6. Establishing the criteria to be used for determining the acceptability of the risks inherent in the options available is the most important step as these criteria should embody all the views of what is acceptable. This concept is returned to in many places in the chapters that follow but we are focusing here on factors which might determine the criteria of risk acceptability in manufacturing; Fig. 7 identifies the set of leading factors of the type that could make the project unacceptable.

The decision-maker should be able to specify, in probability terms, the degree of risk that would cause the project to fail. For example, it might be that a 1 in 1000 chance of the project becoming unprofitable within five years would be acceptable but that a 1 in 100 chance of it becoming unprofitable within that timescale would be unacceptable. The precise figure adopted in such an assessment will be determined by the extent to which the decision-maker is a risk taker or is risk averse.

It is often the case that hard, quantitative evidence on which to base a decision is not available; in such cases, decisions will have to be based on qualitative opinions. Even so, provided that the opinions are collected in a carefully structured and consistent way, it should be possible to postulate the magnitude of the risk at the outset and to refine the estimate, using Bayesian techniques, as the project proceeds.

Once a project has been embarked upon it becomes increasingly difficult to stop — despite any risks which may become manifest; in such cases, what normally happens is that the project becomes modified in some way to make it more acceptable, but this generally increases costs and introduces delays.

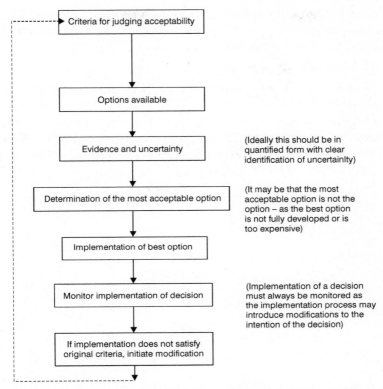

Fig. 6. Structure of the methodology for determining acceptable risk in manufacturing projects

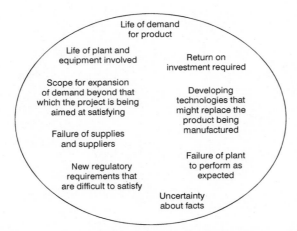

Fig. 7. Outline composition of the manufacturing risk acceptability criteria set

From the above discussions one can draw the following conclusions about the optimum methodology for assessing the acceptability of the risks associated with a manufacturing project.

- The acceptability of the risks must be judged against clearly defined criteria that take into account the decision-maker's view of what is an acceptable risk.
- Determination of the risks associated with a particular proposition must take into account all the risks involved with the proposition; leaving out some risk factor can give a misleading impression of the acceptability of the spectrum of risk involved.

4

Risks in the financial sector

In this chapter, risks in the financial sector are examined in four ways: basic composition of financial decisions; assessing repeat decisions; decisions involving a degree of novelty; uncertainties and how to deal with them. By examining the financial sector in this way, the parameters that are generally taken as measures of an organisation's financial health are first identified. Next, the differences between otherwise similar projects are examined with the aim of identifying the financial consequences of such differences. The third part of the chapter examines the nature of the financial problems that a novel project introduces. Finally, the sources of financial uncertainties in various types of project are examined and the problems involved in arriving at an estimate of the total financial uncertainty in a project are discussed.

The financial sector is involved with taking risks it considers to be acceptable and at a price that will give an adequate return. Both the terms *acceptable risk* and *adequate return* have many shades of meaning. But, in general terms, an acceptable risk in the financial sector is one that, allowing for uncertainty, yields a positive return for the investor. This definition agrees with the definition of risk given in chapter 2, and fits both the banking and the insurance parts of the financial sector. An adequate return is judged by comparison with the alternative investment options open. Some investment options may offer a lower return but with a very predictable frequency of payment. Other investments may offer a higher return but there may be considerable uncertainty about what the return will be and when it will be received. Sometimes this unpredictability is referred to as volatility, but we prefer to keep the number of terms used to a minimum and just use the term uncertainty, as it captures the essence of the argument we want to develop. In addition, we recognise that there are occasions when two options offer the same return and the same degree of uncertainty. On such occasions the decision about which option to accept is a problem that tends to be settled in a somewhat arbitrary way. It is a problem that is returned to later in this chapter and in the chapters that follow.

Although the nature of financial risks may be illustrated in many ways, insurance of the risk of natural catastrophes gives a considerable insight into the underlying risk acceptability philosophy of the financial sector as a whole. In the 1990s, higher losses due to natural disasters were experienced than had ever been experienced before. Of particular concern to the insurance industry was the fact that not only had the frequency of natural catastrophes increased but also the average loss per event had increased.[31] Part of the increase in loss was the result of population growth and the concentration of value in disaster-prone regions. It was estimated that in the United States of America the gap between cover and potential loss was 30 billion US dollars.[32] From the philosophical point of view, it is important to recognise the solution that was adopted. The industry did not walk away from the risk with the excuse that they would not accept that form of risk, instead they looked at other ways of funding the cover. In other words, the situation was still within their risk acceptability philosophy. The solutions adopted included defining earthquake risk bands and issuing insurance derivatives.

Although the ultimate decision about the acceptability of risk may be made on a subjective basis by the decision-maker, growing use is being made of assessment methodologies that are based on quantitative or at least ordinal based methods of ranking the acceptability of risks. It must be understood that while some decisions are concerned with situations that are repeats of situations that have been dealt with before and for which sound quantitative evidence has been built up, many decisions have some degree of novelty. It is the novelty involved that is the most difficult to deal with. Although some attention is given in this chapter to decisions related to repeat decisions based on hard quantitative evidence, most attention is given to decisions that include an element of novelty and have to be based on qualitative evidence. Novelty may arise in many ways, including changes in technology, changes in the working and living environment, changes in political structure and changes in economic structure.

Basic composition of financial decisions

The title of this section suggests that there is a basic composition of all financial decisions, but that is only partly true. What is true is that financial institutions are ultimately concerned to identify in money terms the benefit to them of being involved in some project or activity. Central to this concern for a bank is assessment of their client's ability to repay any loan made to them and to pay interest on the loan. A really bad decision for a bank is one that ultimately results in them having to write off a loan. Such events do happen with all types of loans that banks make. In a similar way, the insurance industry is concerned to establish how real the risks are that they are asked to cover and the adequacy of the premium that market conditions dictate that they can charge.

Banks may assess the acceptability of credit risks in several ways. Although each bank will have its own preferred method, which may be computerised such as Credit Metrics,[33] the essential feature of credit risk assessment is identification of the type of client. The types of client a bank might have to deal with can be divided into three broad categories: individual; company; country. The suitability of an individual for a loan is likely to be rated on income and security for repayment that can be offered. The relationship between security and size of loans permitted varies between lending institutions and countries. Typically, security for a loan to an individual could be house, car, insurance policy or stocks and shares.

In assessing the acceptability of making a loan to a company a bank might evaluate about 50 parameters, a sample of which is given in Table 12. They may summarise the significance of the parameters under three headings; typically the headings used are historical performance, dividend policy and transparency. The assessment under the three headings is brought together to give an overall rating on a three-point scale, often being A, B and C. A is high and C is low. As will be shown later, some scales used for rating the risks perceived to be associated with a company are very much larger than three points. Attention is drawn to the importance attached to transparency. The kind of transparency referred to is openness of financial reporting, in other words do published reports make clear the real situation. This transparency of reporting applies both to the internal and external reporting. For example, would it have been possible to predict the collapse of British and Commonwealth, the Bank of Credit and Commerce, and Barings from the reports they published immediately prior to their collapse? The need for transparency is an easy requirement to state, but in practice it is difficult to satisfy and even more difficult to prove that it has been satisfied.

Table 12. Composition of financial report assessment ratio groups

Ratio group	Component ratios		
Activity ratios	Inventory turnover	=	$\dfrac{\text{Sales}}{\text{Inventory}}$
	Fixed asset turnover	=	$\dfrac{\text{Sales}}{\text{Net fixed assets}}$
	Total asset turnover	=	$\dfrac{\text{Sales}}{\text{Total assets}}$
Cost structure ratios	Gross profit margin	=	$\dfrac{\text{Sales less cost of sales}}{\text{Sales}}$
	Selling expense ratio	=	$\dfrac{\text{Selling expense}}{\text{Sales}}$
	General cost ratio	=	$\dfrac{\text{General and admin. cost}}{\text{Sales}}$
	Depreciation plus lease and rental costs ratio	=	$\dfrac{\text{Depreciation plus lease and rental costs}}{\text{Sales}}$
Leverage ratios	Leverage ratio	=	$\dfrac{\text{Total debt}}{\text{Total assets}}$
	Fixed charge coverage ratio	=	$\dfrac{\text{Income available for meeting fixed charges}}{\text{Fixed charges}}$
	Before-tax income required for sinking final payment	=	$\dfrac{\text{Sinking final payment}}{1 \cdot 0 - \text{Tax rate}}$
Liquidity ratios	Current ratio	=	$\dfrac{\text{Current assets}}{\text{Current liabilities}}$
	Working capital	=	$\dfrac{\text{Current assets} - \text{Current liabilities}}{}$
	Quick ratio	=	$\dfrac{\text{Current assets} - \text{Inventories}}{\text{Current liabilities}}$
Profitability ratios	Profit margin on gross revenue	=	$\dfrac{\text{Net income}}{\text{Gross income}}$
	Return on investment	=	$\dfrac{\text{Net income} + \text{Interest}}{\text{Total assets}}$
	Return on net worth	=	$\dfrac{\text{Net income}}{\text{Net worth}}$

Dun and Bradstreet, the international business information company, claim one factor that gives quite a good indication of the viability of a company is the length of time they take to pay their bills. The gradual extension of the time taken to settle accounts may be taken as a sure sign that a company is heading for financial difficulties, perhaps even bankruptcy.

Another method that is claimed to be 90% accurate in predicting financial problems is the so-called Z-score model.[34] The general form of the Z-score model is

$$Z = 1 \cdot 2x_1 + 1 \cdot 4x_2 + 3 \cdot 3x_3 + 0 \cdot 6x_4 + x_5$$

where

x_1 is
$$\frac{\text{(Current assets} - \text{Current liabilities)}}{\text{Total assets}}$$

x_2 is
$$\frac{\text{Retained earnings}}{\text{Total assets}}$$

x_3 is
$$\frac{\text{Earnings before interest and taxes}}{\text{Total assets}}$$

x_4 is
$$\frac{\text{Market value of preferred and common equity}}{\text{Total debits}}$$

x_5 is
$$\frac{\text{Sales}}{\text{Total assets}}$$

A firm with a Z-score below 1·8 is considered to be heading for bankruptcy. While the method has much to commend it for assessing the financial status of a company that has been operating for some years, it does not help with assessing the financial stability of a new company. Nor does the method make any allowance for the general economic environment. It may be that different weighting factors can be accepted in a time of deep recession and that there could be some flexibility in the 1·8 score being an alarm signal for imminent bankruptcy.

For a new company without any trading record, or a special partnership just established to build or run one project, a detailed business plan would be called for and the proprietor's experience, capability and background investigated. In both the case of a new small company and a new partnership a bank is likely to call for some kind of security or guarantee for any loan it makes, just like lending to an individual. The security may be deposit of shares, a life insurance policy or call on the proprietor's property. Also the bank will expect to be kept informed about the company's trading performance. Some of the financial ratios that the financial institutions will examine in order to establish the strength of a company are shown in Table 12.

Simply considering one year's ratios may be misleading; a better indication is given by examining the trends in a company's performance. By considering several years it will be possible to identify the validity of a company's performance. Volatility is an important characteristic of a company's performance. Understanding volatility or the cyclic nature of a company's business prevents judgements being made on the basis of one good or one bad year.

Some analysts have recently been using 15 cause and effect ratios (Table 13). Some of these ratios are very similar to the financial statement ratios described in Table 12. Taken together, the ratios give a good indication of the past performance of a company, but it must be stressed that they only relate to the past performance. Because the ratios are calculated from financial statements they tend to be out of date and past performance is not always a reliable indicator of current or future performance.

If a bank is considering a loan to a company in another country, the bank would include in its evaluation the country's economic position and its political stability. A typical range of factors considered are shown in Table 14. Each factor may require a detailed study: for example assessing the risks associated with the political situation may involve assessment of the ideology of political leaders, identification of the existence of social unrest and the nationality of the parent company. Other factors that might have to be considered are

- whether the market for the country's main products is increasing or decreasing
- variations in exchange rates
- the influence of inflation on the real interest rates.

These factors are considered in more detail by Clark and Marois.[35]

The significance of each factor could be described in simple, qualitative terms such as unchanged or improving. The final judgement about acceptability is made by an experienced assessor on the basis of experience. Alternatively, the significance of the factors could be ranked on an ordinal basis, the numerical value of the ranking giving an indication of acceptability. Care has to be taken on the design of the ranking scale to ensure that good rankings are not swamped by bad rankings, and bad rankings are not swamped by good rankings. This problem is considered further in the section on uncertainties and how to deal with them.

Table 13. Cause and effect ratios

Ratio group	Component ratio		
Causal ratios	Inventory turnover	=	$\dfrac{\text{Net sales}}{\text{Inventory}}$
	Profit objective	=	$\dfrac{\text{Net profits}}{\text{Net sales}}$
	Recurables analysis	=	$\dfrac{\text{Current accounts recurable}}{\text{Longest credit terms}}$
	Use of capital	=	$\dfrac{\text{Fixed assets}}{\text{Net worth}}$
	Trading ratio	=	$\dfrac{\text{Net sales}}{\text{Net worth}}$
	Evaluation of assets classification	=	$\dfrac{\text{Miscellaneous assets}}{\text{Net worth}}$
Effect ratios	Current ratio	=	$\dfrac{\text{Current assets}}{\text{Current liabilities}}$
	Current liability ratio	=	$\dfrac{\text{Current liabilities}}{\text{Net worth}}$
	Total liability ratio	=	$\dfrac{\text{Total liabilities}}{\text{Net worth}}$
	Inventory ratio	=	$\dfrac{\text{Inventory}}{\text{Working capital}}$
	Receivable ratio	=	$\dfrac{\text{Trade receivable}}{\text{Working capital}}$
	Long-term liabilities ratio	=	$\dfrac{\text{Long-term liabilities}}{\text{Working capital}}$
	Net profit ratio	=	$\dfrac{\text{Net profit}}{\text{Net worth}}$
	Net sales, ratio 1	=	$\dfrac{\text{Net sales}}{\text{Fixed assets}}$
	Net sales, ratio 2	=	$\dfrac{\text{Net sales}}{\text{Working capital}}$

Three examples of ranking are the Moody, Standard and Poor (S&P) and the institutional investor scales. How these ranking scales relate to the degree of risk is shown in Table 15.[36]

The use of a 100 point scale for the institutional investor scale suggests that the assessor can differentiate risks on a 100 point scale. Can an assessor really differentiate between a 95 rating and a 96 rating? How Moody's and S & P's creditworthiness ratings for 134 countries in September 1996 compared with the institutional investor rating is shown in Table 16. It should be noted that the institutional investor rating scale does produce some ratings that are at the margin of the range for each category of risk.

A financial institution's judgement of the magnitude of the risk involved will be manifest in the interest charged on any loan made. The general relationship between interest charged and risk is shown in Fig. 8. At the low risk level would be loans such as between banks. At the high end of the risk spectrum would be unsecured loans like those available to users of credit cards. In fact, comparing credit card interest rates with mortgage rates gives a good indication of the relationship between risk and interest rate charged.

The presentation so far has been mainly concerned with the situation as it is in private industry. The situation becomes rather different if government finance is involved. There are many financial institutions around the world that are established to provide finance for various kinds of projects using funds that are in some way derived, at least partly,

Table 14. Factors considered in assessing the risks of a loan to another country

Factors	Parameter used to judge risk
Domestic economy	Real GDP growth %
	Investment GDP (international average 25%)
	Investment efficiency (critical level <0·2)
	Inflation %
	Money supply growth %
	Real domestic credit creation %
	Fiscal balance/GDP %
External economy	Competitive index (compared to base year)
	Trade balance (goods)
	Exports (goods and services)
	Imports (goods and services)
	Current account balance
	Exports/GDP %
	Export concentration
Debt characteristics	Total external debt (public and private)
	International reserves excluding gold
	External debt service
	External debt/exports (critical level >150%)
	External debt service/exports (critical level >25%)
	Interest adjusted current account/interest payments
	International reserves/imports
Socio-political factors	Political risk (ranked on a scale)
	Recorded unemployment rate
	Per capita GDP grow

Table 15. Moody, S & P and institutional investor risk ranking

Grade	Risk	Moody	S&P	Institutional investor
Investment	Low	Aaa	AAA	100–86
		Aa1	AA+	85–81
		Aa2	AA	809–76
		Aa3	AA–	75–71
		A1	A+	70–66
	Medium	A2	A	65–61
		A3	A–	60–56
		Baa1	BBB+	55–51
		Baa2	BBB	50–46
		Baa3	BBB–	45–41
Speculative	High	Ba1	BB+	40–37
		Ba2	BB	36–33
		Ba3	BB–	32–29
		B1	B+	28–26
		B2	B	25–23
		B3	B–	22–20
		Caa	CCC	19–17
		Ca	CC	16–14
		C	C	13–11
			D	10–0

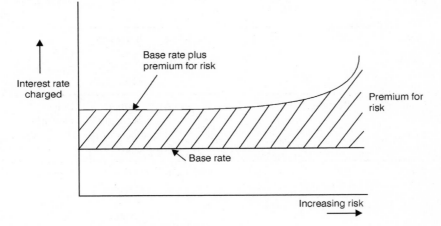

Fig. 8. Relation of interest charged to risk

Table 16 (below, facing and overleaf). Country creditworthiness rating

A. *Investment grade*

Moody	S&P	Institutional investor range from Table 15	Institutional investor	Ranking of country range	
Aaa	AAA	100–86	100–85·6	Austria France Germany Japan	Luxembourg Netherlands Switzerland United Kingdom
Aa1	AA+	85–81	85·5–80·6	Denmark Norway Singapore	
Aa2	AA	80–76	80·5–75·6	Belgium Canada	Taiwan
Aa3	AA–	75–71	75·5–70·6	Australia Finland Ireland Italy	New Zealand South Korea Spain Sweden
A1	A+	70–66	70·5–65·6	Malaysia	Portugal
A2	A	65–61	65·5–60·6	Chile Czech Republic Hong Kong	Malta Thailand United Arab Emirates
A3	A–	60–56	60·5–55·6	China Cyprus	Iceland
Baa1	BBB+	55–51	55·5–50·6	Indonesia Israel Kuwait Mauritius	Oman Qatar Saudi Arabia
Baa2	BBB	50–46	50·5–45·6	Bahrain Botswana Colombia Greece	India Slovenia South Africa
Baa3	BBB–	45–41	45·5–40·6	Barbados Hungary Mexico Poland	Slovakia Tunisia Turkey

Table 16 — continued

B. Speculative grade

Moody	S&P	Institutional investor range from Table 15	Institutional investor	Ranking of country range	
Ba1	BB+	40–37	40·5–36·6	Argentina Brazil Morocco	Philippines Trinidad and Tobago Uruguay
Ba2	BB	36–33	36·5–32·6	Costa Rica Egypt Jordan	Papua New Guinea Sri Lanka Vietnam
Ba3	BB–	32–29	32·5–28·6	Estonia Ghana Pakistan Paraguay Peru	Romania Swaziland Venezuela Zimbabwe
B1	B+	28–26	28·5–25·6	Bangladesh Croatia Ecuador Gabon Jamaica Kenya	Latvia Lebanon Libya Nepal Panama Seychelles
B2	B	25–23	25·5–22·6	Algeria Bolivia Bulgaria Guatemala	Dominican Republic Iran Lithuania Syria
B3	B–	22–20	22·5–19·6	El Salvador Kazakhstan Malawi	Myanmar (Burma) Russia Senegal
Caa	CCC	19–17	19·5–16·6	Benin Burkina Faso Cameroon Cote d'lvoire Honduras	Mali Tanzania Togo Ukraine

Table 16 — continued

Moody	S&P	Institutional investor range from Table 15	Institutional investor	Ranking of country range	
Ca	CC	16–14	16·5–13·6	Albania Belarus Congo Ethiopia Guinea	Mozambique Nigeria Uganda Uzbekistan Zambia
C	C	13–11	13·5–10·6	Angola Cuba	Grenada Nicaragua
	D	10–0	10·5–0	Afghanistan Georgia Haiti Iraq Liberia	North Korea Sierra Leone Sudan Yugoslavia Zaire

from government sources. These institutions may use criteria to judge the suitability for support that are quite different from the criteria used by financial institutions in the private sector.

For example, lending might be motivated mainly by socio-political interests rather than by strict economic criteria. Money might be given interest free to an undeveloped country to encourage it to develop industries that will help the country improve its gross domestic product. Similarly, funds might be given to an ex-communist country to help it solve some chronic environmental problem such as large dumps of toxic or radioactive waste that have been allowed to build up over the years.

Another variation of the use of public funds is the form of joint public and private funding. In such cases the assessment of the suitability of the project for funding may take more the form of the private industry approach already described. But the findings of the private industry assessment may be overridden by socio-political considerations of doubtful value. Private industry being content to join the venture if it is given some form of guarantee that any losses it makes will be covered by the government.

This leads to the question — is the efficacy of expenditure of public funds effectively assessed in a transparent way? The answer to this question is outside the scope of this book, but it is a question that must be considered by everyone involved in allocating public funds.

Repeat decisions

The first question that must be answered in considering a proposal about the acceptability of what appears to be a repeat decision is — can any two decisions be exactly alike? It is very doubtful that any two decisions can be exactly alike in every detail. The loans officer in a bank might be faced with two customers in one morning both wanting loans of £20 000. Superficially, both involve the same type of decision for a loan of £20 000. Looking a little more closely at the two proposals, one man may be earning £100 000 a year and be expecting a bonus of £25 000 in three months time, which would allow him to pay off the loan in three months. The other man may have a small taxi business, with a somewhat variable income, and want the money to replace one of his taxis. In the past he has had trouble repaying smaller loans to the agreed schedule. It is easy to see that the loans officer might be willing to make a loan to the first man and have doubts about giving a loan to the second man.

Before moving to more complex decisions it is important to note that in some situations, experienced loans officers have been found to have a fairly high success rate (74%) in predicting the failure of companies and a majority decision from a group of assessors improved the accuracy to 82%.[37] This does not mean that a high success rate can be attributed to every financial decision-maker. The decision-making that led to the collapse of Barings Bank and the problems members of Lloyd's of London had due to asbestos claims illustrates the magnitude of the problems that can be associated with financial decision-making.

More complex financing will be involved in projects such as a large building, development of a new medical drug, expanding a factory making car components, building a Ro-Ro ferry, building a privately financed rail tunnel and building a new theatre. The list has been chosen so that it contains projects that may in general terms be repeated. Many large buildings are built, many new drugs are developed, several car component factories are built, many Ro-Ro ferries are built, several rail tunnels are constructed and several new theatres are built. The list has also been chosen to include projects that are mainly privately financed or if public money is involved, it is only in amounts that are not significant to the main decision-making process.

The nature of the similarities and kind of factors that can make differences between otherwise similar projects are summarised in Table 17. Essentially, the differences identified are related to the technical conditions surrounding the project and the way the project is financed. To put the possibility of cost overruns into perspective, it should be noted that in 1992 the UK government's National Audit Office reported that average

47

Table 17. Some of the features that may cause otherwise similar projects to have different financial implications

Project	Similarities	Differences that may cause problems
Large building	Building the same size and design	Consortium providing finance goes bankrupt because it has not sufficient funds to finance detailed changes in design
Development of a new medical drug	Basically a new use for an existing drug	Clinical testing of drug for new use shows drug has side effects not detected in testing for earlier use; this endangers all applications of drug
Expanding a factory to make car components	Components to be produced the same as made in existing factory	Customers for new components demand higher reliability of components and more competitive price
Building a Ro-Ro ferry	Same design and size proposed as existing ferries	Following the loss of several Ro-Ro ships, new regulations were introduced that require new designs to have a long period of testing to prove that they satisfy the regulations
Building a privately financed rail tunnel	Tunnel similar in size and length to tunnels already in service	The stability of the ground is very much less than in previous tunnels — consequently the design and method of construction has to be modified
Building a new theatre	Similar in size to an existing theatre	Financial support uncertain. Many cite specific building restrictions that make design difficult; also the design has to overcome noise and vibration from a nearby underground railway

cost overruns in 1988–89 were 28%.[38] Overspend figures as high as 50% for many major projects have been reported.[39] But it must be remembered that for some notable projects massive overspends have been reported: for example, the Sydney Opera House and Concorde both cost about 10 times the original estimate, and the Thames Barrier cost 20 times the original estimate.[40] These figures give an indication of the variation in risk that can be associated with major construction projects.

The way construction costs may escalate is well illustrated by the failures that can be experienced in tunnelling projects. In a recent review of the various forms of failure that can occur, 14 modes of failure were identified.[41] Table 18 lists 39 major tunnelling disasters that were experienced with one tuneling method between 1973 and 1994. It is also suggested that in Japan there were 71 incidents with this tunnelling method between 1978 and 1991. The advice on how to achieve an essentially failure-free tunnelling operation is applicable to most types of project, and is as follows.

● Assess carefully all the operating conditions involved.
● Select the most appropriate working method and equipment.
● Plan in advance how to deal with all possible contingencies.

The status of the economic environment may have a dramatic influence on the nature of the risks associated with any project or activity; it is not just the variation in supply and demand but the general confidence of the financial market. There are many examples in the past where financial crises have had a major influence on economic confidence in general. These crises have been both at the company level and at the international level. Examples of crises at the company level include Metallgesellschaft (1994), Barings (1995) and Daiwa (1995). International crises have a long history and include Tulipmania (1634), Mississippi Bubble (1720), the Crash of 1929 and the Crash of 1987. Metallgesellschaft bought huge hedges in oil futures. The tailspin in oil spot prices in 1993 led to a wave of margin calls producing huge losses for that company. The losses could mainly be attributed to bad judgements due to lack of knowledge about the complex nature of markets and hedging procedures. The Barings and Daiwa crises were due to the irrational behaviour of dealers that were not effectively controlled by their management. (Clear examples of poor risk control.) They could be called crises caused by letting gambling get out of hand.

Tulipmania developed in the early 17th century when tulips became prestige objects of the Dutch bourgeoisie. Rare tulips with special colour

Table 18. Major tunnelling disasters that were experienced with one tunnelling method in the period 1973–1994

Date	Site	Type of failure
Oct. 1973	Paris, railway, France	Collapse
18 Dec. 1981	Sao Paulo Metro, Brazil	Sudden instability
1983	Santana Metro, Brazil	Cave-in
13 Nov. 1984	Landrucken, railway, Germany	Collapse
1984	Bochum Metro 1, Germany	Collapse
17 Jan. 1985	Richtof, railway, Germany	Collapse
1985	Bochum Metro 2, Germany	Collapse
Aug. 1985	Kaiserau, railway, Germany	Collapse
17 Feb. 1986	Krieberg, railway, Germany	Collapse
Before 1987	Munich Metro 1, Germany	Collapse
Before 1987	Munich Metro 2, Germany	Collapse
Before 1987	Munich Metro 3, Germany	Collapse
Before 1987	Munich Metro 4, Germany	Collapse
Before 1987	Munich Metro 5, Germany	Collapse
Before 1987	Munich Metro 6, Germany	Comp. air blowout
Before 1987	Weltkugel, railway, Germany	Cave-in, sandstone
1987	Karawanken, road, Austria/Slovenia	Inflow, rock
Before 1988	Kehrenberg, railway, Germany	Surface settlement
1988	Michaels, Germany	Collapse during enlargement
8 Jan. 1989	Karawanken, road, Austria/Slovenia	Collapse
27 Sep. 1991	Kwachon Metro, Korea	Collapse
17 Nov. 1991	Seoul Metro 1, Korea	Collapse
27 Nov. 1991	Seoul Metro 2, Korea	Collapse
1992	Funagata, road, Japan	Collapse
12 Feb. 1992	Seoul Metro 3, Korea	Collapse
30 Jun. 1992	Lambach, railway, Austria	Collapse
7 Jan. 1993	Seoul Metro 4, Korea	Collapse
2 Feb. 1993	Seoul Metro 5, Korea	Collapse, weathered rock
Feb/Mar. 1993	Seoul Metro 6, Korea	Collapse, weathered rock
Feb/Mar. 1993	Seoul Metro 7, Korea	Collapse
Mar. 1993	Chungho, road, Taiwan	Collapse
Nov. 1993	Sao Paulo, road, Brazil	Collapse
1993	Poggio Fornello, road, Italy	Severe deformation
Apr. 1994	Cardvalho Pinto, road, Brazil	Portal, during repairs
30 Jul. 1994	Montemor, road, Portugal	Collapse, main bore
1 Aug. 1994	Montemor, road, Portugal	Collapse, pilot
Aug. 1994	Galgenberg, road, Austria	Collapse
20 Sept. 1994	Munich Metro, Germany	Collapse
21 Oct. 1994	Heathrow Express, railway, England	Collapse

patterns and shapes brought about by virus infections were very difficult to reproduce. Demand for rare bulbs rose and prices soared to astronomical levels; people sold their houses and valuables to buy the bulbs. In February 1637 panic broke out and prices collapsed, leaving many destitute.

The Mississippi Bubble crisis of 1720 had many speculative characteristics similar to the Tulipmania crisis. In France in the 18th century after the death of Louis XIV the country's economic situation was miserable. In an attempt to solve the problem John Law founded Compagnie d'Occident Banque Generale and several other firms mainly engaged in trade. There was great enthusiasm for the shares and prices rose dramatically, The companies Law founded were not successful and panic broke out as share prices fell. At the end of 1720 John Law had to flee Paris fearing for his life.

The stock market crashes of 1929 and 1987 could be characterised as macroeconomic crises, which were initiated by a surge of destabilising speculation. In the period 1982–1987, share prices in the USA showed an upward trend despite high levels of US budget and current account deficits. Some of the optimism was due to the fact that the USA had quickly overcome the recession triggered by the oil price crisis of 1979/1980. It is claimed that many investors knew that the share prices were overvalued and that they hoped they would be able to get out of the market at its peak. When specialist dealers were not able to deal with the selling pressures and computers were overloaded panic erupted. Share prices fell 22% and many international centres registered large drops in share prices. Banks 'as lenders of last resort' provided liquidity to many firms which reduced the number of company failures. Nevertheless, there were many company failures.

In his elegant analysis of the nature of financial crises, Professor Aschinger categorised crises under four headings, namely microeconomic, macroeconomic, informational and speculative.[42] Table 19 shows how

Table 19. Types of financial crisis

Crisis	Informational	Speculative
Microeconomic	Metallgesellschaft (1994)	Barings (1995) Daiwa (1995)
Macroeconomic		Tulipmania (1634) Mississippi Bubble (1720) Crash (1929) Crash (1987)

he classified the seven cases mentioned earlier. In his analysis he also drew attention to the fact that

> Under normal circumstances speculation reduces price volatility and improves market efficiency. However, speculation can be destabilising if expectations are not fulfilled because of inaccurate information, exaggerations or time lags.

This stresses how dangerous the herd instinct can be.

Six stages can be identified in the development of a speculative crisis; these stages can also be seen to be associated with changes in the risk level. They are

Stage 1   *Displacement*. Explained shock affecting the macroeconomic system.

Stage 2   *Development of boom*. New opportunities outweigh lost opportunities, investment and production pick-up leading to a boom.

Stage 3   *Start of speculation*. Boom condition nourished by expansion of credit. Supply not able to match demand so prices rise. Speculation within predictable limits.

Stage 4   *Destabilising speculation*. Price increases cause speculation to be intensified and market to overreact. A speculative bubble develops.

Stage 5   *Euphoria*. Market becomes dominated by emotional rather than objective thinking. Decisions taken on an irrational basis.

Stage 6   *Panic*. Market instability escalates and prices show an exponential trend. Market becomes fragile. A single almost unimportant piece of information may cause panic selling and collapse of the market.

Aschinger examined the circumstances of the 1987 crash using catastrophe and speculative bubble models. It is inappropriate to go into the mathematics of the two models here, but full details are given in ref. 42. We are convinced that the speculative bubble model has an advantage over the catastrophe model in that it predicted the collapse of the share index well in advance of its real occurrence. However, we are well aware that it is easier to predict future events when you have all the relevant information than to predict the future when only part of the information is available.

These events and the models indicate clearly how market factors may change and change the risk to which an investor is exposed.

In addition, there are a range of socio-political factors that have to be considered. Such factors range from the activities of pressure groups who are opposed to the project to those that support the project. The activities of pressure groups may lead to protracted legal processes such as public inquiries or court cases. The delays and costs involved in such processes may result in the proposer finding a different solution or even cancelling the project.

The activities of pressure groups are not a new phenomenon. For example, there are many towns without direct connection to the railway system, because at the time railways were being built there was opposition from local residents and landowners. There are differences between countries in the influence of pressure groups. The influence of pressure groups is greatest in democracies and least in dictatorships. Even in democracies, governments have sometimes found it necessary to limit the amount of discussion of the acceptability of projects on the grounds that delay would reduce the economic benefit of the project.

Decisions involving a degree of novelty

If there is novelty in a proposal or form of investment there can be no previous experience on which to base an assessment of the acceptability of the risks that are thought to be involved. This dilemma facing the decision-maker is hard to resolve. The way the dilemma is resolved depends to a certain extent on the environment in which the decision-maker works. In Table 20 a number of possible decision-making environments are considered which show something of the range of approaches to decision-making that may be adopted. It is not suggested that any one method is universally acceptable, but the method or combination of methods adopted has to be adapted to the particular project. In essence, the decision-maker has to find a way of determining what is an acceptable risk from the unacceptable risk. The unacceptable risk is the occurrence of a condition that would do irreparable damage to the organisation involved, while an acceptable risk is one that would still leave the proposal of lasting benefit to the proposer.

The central concern of the decision-maker involved in making decisions about the acceptability of a project that is novel is whether or not the novelty introduces a degree of uncertainty into financial calculations that could endanger the financial integrity of the organisation involved.

Uncertainties and how to deal with them

We are not going to suggest that there is some simple mathematical method for dealing with all uncertainties, but we stress that whatever methodology is adopted it must be logically defensible, in keeping with the best traditions of statistical analysis, and transparent. In the analysis of the financial significance of uncertainties, some of the factors that the methodology has to include are

(a)   identification of the variables that are involved
(b)   the magnitude of the variables in money terms

Table 20. Possible decision-making environments

Organisational situation	Financial constraints	Other constraints
Small company proposing development of a new product	The company's financial resources limited and might have to borrow or abandon product if difficulties develop	Demand for existing products falling due to them becoming out of date
Large company proposing to take over a major competitor	Purchase more than company can afford but hopes to balance the books by selling assets of company taken over	Assets of company taken over not as great as had been anticipated
Construction company tendering for a major contract	Is the financial commitment more than the company can withstand? Has the client got the financial resources to cover all contingencies?	The description of the work required given in the request for tender documents is not accurate
A government department proposing to finance a major defence project	The extent of the development work required not clearly identified. The company involved is going to build up a labour force for which there would be no other work if the project is cancelled.	Government policy may change causing project to be scrapped
A government/private consortium proposing to build a series of major motorways	How is the funding to be shared? How investment is to be returned? What are the cash flow implications?	Government policy may change leaving no way of recovering investment
An insurance company proposing to underwrite a factory making a toxic substance by a novel method	No previous experience on which to base premium—can commitment be limited (risk shared)?	Other companies premium hungry, willing to take risk at lower premium

(c)   how the magnitude of the variables is determined (e.g. is the assessment of the magnitude based on the subjective assessment of one person or the collective view of experts?)

(d)   what uncertainties there are in the specification of the project (e.g. are the properties known of all the materials to be used?; are all the people to be involved in the project properly trained and welded into an effective team?)

(e)   how does this project differ from any previously undertaken projects?

How the uncertainties may be associated with these five factors is summarised in Tables 21–25. The relationship between uncertainties and the five factors is dealt with in very general terms in the tables and for any specific project the relationship between uncertainties and factors would have to be tailored to suit the particular project.

To determine the overall uncertainty associated with a project in a simple way, it would be possible to argue that the overall uncertainty is

Table 21. Uncertainties in the identification of the variables involved

Possible variable	Possible uncertainty
Planning approval	How long will it take to get approved, will a public inquiry be involved?
Ground conditions	Are ground conditions known with precision, are any toxic wastes present?
Available finance	Will finance be able to deal with any cost overruns that may arise?
State of financial market	Is the market likely to change dramatically within the life of the proposal? (This could include some allowance for the stage in the development of the speculative bubble mentioned earlier)
Contractors experienced and financially sound	With a novel project contractors may not have relevant experience
Project planned in detail	Detailed planning may expose aspects of the project that have not been effectively considered
Any legislation likely to be introduced that could adversely affect the project	New legislation may delay a project or require it to be radically redesigned
Has a realistic life for the project been defined	Variation in the expected life of a project has a significant impact on costs

Table 22. Uncertainties in the magnitude of the variables

Possible variable	Nature of uncertainty
Labour cost	More work might be required than originally envisaged. During the life of the project there may be inflationary changes in labour costs
Finance costs	Interest rate changes might change cost of finance. Changes in economic conditions might force changes in repayment schedule
Possible delays	Delays are likely to increase all the running cost of the project
Start up costs	Start up procedures may show weakness in concept that will be costly to correct
Shut down costs	When the project reaches the end of its life there might be high shut down costs to consider—such as returning site to green field conditions and removing toxic wastes
Income from project	It might have been assumed that the project would receive some income from its operation—the income might prove to be higher or lower than expected

Table 23. Uncertainties in the determination of the variables

Possible variable	Uncertainties in determination
Performance of design	With a novel design experts may be consulted about the likely performance. Each expert should be consulted in a consistent way so that their opinions are comparable. It may be possible to do a statistical analysis of the opinions expressed
Cost of work	Work required may only be vaguely known
Estimate of income	Estimate of likely demand may be in error so estimate of income doubtful
Predicted running costs	Predicted running costs higher than expected due to unreliability of equipment and operator
Development testing shows trust in design misplaced	Failures of vital components during development testing shows original design concept defective

Table 24. Uncertainties in the specification of the project

Possible variable	Nature of uncertainty
Definition of work to be done	There are gaps in the work specified which mean that the project cannot be completed without the specification being modified. It is not clear that the additional work required can be completed satisfactorily
Arrangements for settling disputes	In the normal course of a project disputes arise between client and contractor. Unless the procedure for settling disputes is clearly defined in the contractual documents additional costs and delays can result
Definition of responsibilities	The specification of a project should define clearly the flow of management responsibilities. These arrangements should be confirmed in the contractual documents for the project, so that both client and contractor understand the arrangements
Proof that the work can be done in the way specified	The success of a project may depend on several components interacting and performing in a particular way. Proof that such components will perform in an acceptable way may require an extensive testing programme. The success of the project may depend on the components completing their test programme in a satisfactory way
Proof that finance is available to pay for the work specified	The total funding of the project may be built up from funds from several sources. Not all sources may be equally committed to the project. For example, part of the funding may be from government sources that may be subject to the whims of government policy
Confirmation that there is no organised public opposition to the project	Sometimes with major projects there is organised public opposition that can stop or delay a project. Examples of such opposition are attempts to stop work on motorways and opposition to siting chemical or nuclear plants

Table 25. *Uncertainties about how the project differs from previous projects*

Possible variable	Nature of uncertainty
Producing an airliner with double the current level of seating	Airports may not be able to handle such an increase in passenger flow
For a chemical plant, stricter environmental regulations	The additional environmental regulations may increase the cost of the product to such an extent that alternatives become competitive
For a medical drug, more extensive testing for side effects	The development process of the drug may be drawn out for several years
Increased use of derivatives as a way of providing finance for companies	The underlying security may not justify the additional provision of finance so the derivatives market would be irrelevant. However, the derivatives market may destabilise the rest of the financial market
Coupling insurance premiums to the findings of risk assessments	Assumes that there is a fixed relationship between risk and premium. Also there must be concern about how precisely the risks are defined in quantitative terms.
Inspection and testing not adequate to identify latent defects	Latent defects that escape detection by the inspection and testing processes used may cause problems many years after the plant, building or equipment has been put into service

$$U_{total} = +U_1 +U_2 +U_3 +U_4 +U_5 \qquad (4.1)$$

where U_1 is the uncertainty due to errors in the identification of the variables involved

U_2 is the uncertainty due to the magnitude of the variables involved

U_3 is the uncertainty in determination of the variable

U_4 is the uncertainty in the specification of the project

U_5 is the uncertainty in how the project differs from previous projects.

There are five problems in converting equation (4.1) into quantitative terms. They are

(a) Is the effect of the uncertainty positive or negative?

(b) What units are the uncertainties measured in? (It has to be recognised that the magnitude of the uncertainty could be expressed in some ordinal form.)

(c) The existence of some form of uncertainty may go undetected.

(d) Do the uncertainties have some identifiable statistical distribution?

(e) Has double counting been avoided estimating the variables and their magnitude?

When it is difficult to identify and quantify an uncertainty it may be acceptable to adopt a comparative method. Such a method would consist of comparing the proposed project with some similar completed project and then assessing whether each uncertainty associated with the proposed project was likely to be greater than, less than or equal to the uncertainty in the completed project. The extent of the deviation of the proposed project uncertainty from the completed project uncertainty could be expressed in the form of some ordinal ranking scales.

However, if acceptability of the project is just being judged in financial terms an attempt should be made to put the uncertainties in consistent money terms. For example, the final cost of the project is estimated as being in the range $£x \pm U_{total}$ where x is the best estimate of total cost and U_{total} is the overall uncertainty as defined in equation (4.1).

A specific example of how organisations in the financial sector attempt to deal with potential risks is given by the way they estimate the provision that should be made for unexpected losses on their overall loan portfolio.[43] The possible loss on a loan portfolio depends on the sum of the risk characteristics of each individual transaction. Three dimensions are considered

(a) the risk that a borrower will not be able to meet his obligations

(b) the exposure which the bank will have at that point in time

(c) the percentage actually lost after realising collateral or instituting collection proceedings against the customer.

The biggest value driver is the first dimension, the statistical probability of default by the customer. Measurement of this risk may be based on independent studies such as by rating agencies, which have tracked companies and their defaults over many years, and internal analyses of the organisation's own loss experience. In day-to-day business, based on credit analyses, organisations allocate customers an individual rating which has a given statistical probability of default. This can be illustrated by a simplified example.

From an analysis of the records of 1000 clients of similar size and activity an institution finds that, on average over an economic cycle, 10 per year have defaulted on their obligations. This means that the statistical default risk is 1%. While it is expected that 10 out of 1000 companies will get into financial difficulties, it is not known which they will be. The institution, therefore, has to expect that all of them individually have a 1% probability of default. If the exposure is the same in all cases, for example £200 000, and the recovery rate of those that get into difficulties is 50%, this results in an expected loss of £1 million per year, which the institution offsets by charging a credit risk premium of £1 000 per customer. If the expected 10 loans all go into default, the bank will only lose half of the £2 million loss as £1 million will be provided by the credit risk premium. If 12 clients actually go bankrupt instead of 10 the effective loss would grow to £1·2 million. Of this, £1 million would be financed by the credit risk premium leaving £0·2 million uncovered as a so-called unexpected loss.

More formally, the approach financial institutions adopt to make provision for dealing with the risk of loss is to adopt what is euphemistically called the *Insurance approach*.[44] Typically, about half the losses expected will be regarded as a predictable cost of doing business, such losses being funded from net profits. Then there will be losses occurring less than once in 40 years, such losses will be covered by Actuarial Credit Risk Accounting (ACRA) reserve. (Once in 40 years is only a national figure, each institution will fix its own frequency limit.) Other losses will have to be absorbed by reserves/equity capital. The acceptable probability of predictable financial loss is often higher than the acceptable probability of loss of life.

The important conclusion that this examination of risks in the financial sector seems to justify is: the financial sector has developed a philosophy of accepting a certain level of risk. To determine what is an acceptable risk the financial sector has developed a pragmatic approach, conditioned by experience, that evaluates the parameters that they consider to be important in determining the acceptability of the risks they are faced with.

5

Major project risks

There are four main parts to this chapter. The first part identifies a number of major project failures that illustrate the range of risk factors that have to be considered in either assessing the likely success of a project or organising a project in a way that minimises the risk of failure. The second part of the chapter sets out the spectrum of factors that should be considered in evaluating the acceptability of the risks associated with a project. The third part deals with the evaluation of risks. The fourth part introduces a methodology for assessment and uncertainties in risk assessment.

Major project failures

We can all recall projects that have failed, been cancelled or involved massive overspends. Under the heading of failed, cancelled and problem projects come projects such as Canvey Island, the Channel Tunnel, the Sydney Opera House, the San Francisco Bay Rapid Transport System (BART), Thames Barrier, Comet Airliner, Nimrod, Airships and TSR2.[45] The collapse in October 1994 of the tunnels for the Heathrow Express at Heathrow resulted in serious problems for that project.[46] Although the list contains several aircraft projects, it is clear that aircraft projects are not the only risky undertakings. A list of tunnelling disasters was given in Table 18 in chapter 4. A sample of civil engineering projects that have had problems is given in appendix 2. However, as the failure of aircraft projects are often well written up and explained in the open literature, it is generally easier to extract from their case histories important lessons about the nature of the risk problems inherent in any project. Table 26 lists some important aircraft projects that have failed

Table 26. Some major British aircraft projects that have failed [47]

Aircraft	Duration of project	Expenditure	Reason for failure
Comet airliner	Entered service 1952, crashes in 1954 showed design flawed		Fatigue life of cabin not properly investigated before the aircraft went into service. Correction of the defect resulted in the market being lost.
Nimrod AEW (intended as a replacement for the Shackleton AEW 3, and to make use of Comet design and experience)	10 years	£900 million [48, 49]	The American Sentry AEW was judged to be cheaper and a proven alternative; available more quickly
TSR2	6 years 4 months	Cost to the taxpayer estimated to be at least £250 million [50]	Cost of project and opposition from influential government adviser who was not a specialist in aircraft design or engineering
Manchester (WW2 Bomber)	Prototype flew July 1939, last built 1941		Only 200 built as it was bedevilled by frequent failure of the Rolls Royce Vulture engine. Modified to take four Merlin engines, it became the successful Lancaster bomber [51]
Princess Flying Boat (weight 300 000 lb) [52]	First flew 1952		Underpowered — the ten Bristol Proteus engines did not develop sufficient power and overtaken by land based jetliners
Brabazon [53]	1942–1952		Started life in 1942 as a concept for a long range bomber. The novel feature of the design was that the engines were buried in the wings to reduce drag and were coupled in pairs driving four sets of propellers. The version that was built was intended to carry 180 passengers. The prototype flew in September 1949. The project was cancelled in February 1952 before entering service partly because the airframe was considered to have a limited life

and includes some of the important reasons for their failure. It is also appreciated that there have been some very successful aircraft projects that have yielded substantial profits for their makers, but the failures sometimes give more information than successes about problems to be solved.

A broader spectrum of failures is identified in Table 27 and shows how often failure resulting from the non-meeting of technical targets leads to economic failure. It should also be noted that failure at one time does not necessarily mean permanent failure. Many bridges have been built since the Tay Bridge disaster and 30 years after the original problems with the thalidomide drug, researchers were looking for other possible uses for it. The Rolls Royce RB211 engine case shows most of the characteristics of project failure/recovery situations.

The Rolls Royce RB211 story starts in the 1960s when development of the engine to replace the Conway engine started.[47] The incentive to develop the engine was that Rolls Royce's main competitors, General Electric and Pratt and Whitney in America, had started to develop larger engines for the next generation of large aircraft. After long and difficult negotiations in March 1968, Rolls Royce obtained an order from Lockheed for 450 of the RB211–22 version of the engine. The estimated launching cost was £100 million. The British Government offered aid of £47·13 million for launching costs from August 1967. The aid was to be repaid on the sales of the engines.

Development of the engine continued throughout 1968 and 1969 and it became clear that the company had underestimated the magnitude of the problems to be overcome in developing the RB211. One example of the problems was that too few experienced design engineers were assigned to the project. During 1970 the situation got out of control and the company ran into severe financial difficulties in developing the engine to satisfy the Lockheed contract. In November 1970 the Government agreed to increase its launching aid and banks provided £18 million in loans. The Government financing was subject to an independent audit of the company's affairs. The chairman and chief executive Sir Denning Pearson resigned and Lord Cole became chairman.

In January 1971 Lord Cole reported to the Ministry of Aviation that the development and delivery promised for the production of engines for Lockheed could not be met and there would have to be a postponement of at least six months and perhaps even twelve months. At least another £150 million was required to cover cash flow problems and potential penalty claims for late delivery. After consideration of the situation the Government decided in February 1971 that a receiver had to be appointed

Table 27. Some failures from a broad spectrum of activities

Case	Nature of failure
Superphenix fast breeder reactor	Cost per kilowatt of electricity produced was considered to be astronomical[54]
Plan Calcul (This was a programme designed to prevent the computer industry in France being dominated by IBM or CRAY)	The view has been expressed that for 20 years the programme squandered billions of French francs as a result of poor management[54]
First Tay rail bridge failure	Completed February 1878, failed in a storm 28 December 1879. All 75 people in a train going over the bridge died when the bridge collapsed. Allowance for wind loadings was not as high as used in France or America at the time[55]
Wind turbines	Cracked blades and damaged generators resulted in some turbines being shut down. The price of electricity from renewable energy sources such as wind power makes it non-competitive with electricity from fossil fuels. Demand for wind turbines was half some earlier estimates[56]
Thalidomide	A powerful sedative sold in the early 1960s resulted in the birth of about 10 000 deformed babies. The drug continued to be used as a treatment for leprosy. In 1995, it was reported that the drug was being tested as a way of dealing with a range of diseases including tuberculosis and several AIDS related illnesses[57]
The death of Lake Erie	This event was an important link in the chain of events that led eventually to the identification of the devastating hormone-disrupting effect some chemicals can have in producing abnormalities and reducing fertility. In June 1969, pollution was so bad that the Cuyahoga river that flows into Lake Erie caught fire. Since then, pollution has been reduced and some natural life has returned to the area as a consequence of various factors: local communities have built sewage works; discharges from industries have been reduced; the use of DDT has been restricted[58]

to protect the interests of debenture holders. In other words, the development of the engine had bankrupted the company.

The Government passed legislation to enable it to acquire the assets of the company and keep it going in the interest of national defence. But the Government accepted no liability for the contract between Rolls Royce and Lockheed for the supply of RB211 engines.

In September 1971, the US Government guaranteed credits for Lockheed and later in the month a contract was signed between Lockheed and Rolls Royce that cleared the way for work on the development and production of the RB211 to continue. The cost to the British Government of the rescue operation has been put at between £120 and £195 million. In 1977, the company became a private company again. By mid-1978, 555 RB211 engines had been produced. In the period 1975–1979, Rolls Royce undertook nearly £3000 million worth of aero-engine work of which £1025 million was for the supply of new aero-engines. This example clearly illustrates the risks involved in embarking on a major development without adequate financial and suitably skilled human resources.

Before moving to the more general nature of project failure, it is important to recognise the special characteristics of the problems with military projects. Morris made a detailed review of many major projects.[59] He reported a series of studies of military projects made in the early 1970s which showed cost overruns ranging from 0–700%. The cause of the overruns was attributed to

- the complexity of the projects
- changes in specification
- the fact that no contractor was appointed with overall control of the whole project, consequently contractors tended to work in an uncoordinated way and followed their own interests
- progress was not kept under a systematic review.

From the cases considered several, but not all, of the characteristic causes of project failure can be identified. One important potential cause of failure, not mentioned, is when a contractor has to accept some novel form of contract. Such contracts include the partnership type contracts increasingly used in local government, privatisation contracts and design, build, finance and operate (DBFO) contracts proposed by government.[60] These novel contracts introduce a wide range of risks that have to be carefully considered. The causes are identifiable in civil or military projects and are summarised in Table 28. The causes identified indicate the range of risk factors that have to be evaluated before any project is accepted to determine whether or not it represents an acceptable portfolio risk.

Table 28. Typical causes of project failure

Typical cause of failure	Possible ways of avoiding failure
Client changes his mind about the need for project	Careful assessment of concept and need for project before start
Client has insufficient funds to complete the project	Precontract assessment of client's financial viability. If funding fails during life of project find alternative sources of funding
Decision process takes so long demand for project dies away	Before getting involved in a project agree to a decision-making procedure that is short enough to avoid significant risk of changes in demand
Technical criteria set cannot be satisfied	Before a project is accepted ensure that there is an acceptable chance that the technical criteria specified can be satisfied
Technical criteria set not appropriate to project	Preliminary study to assess adequacy of technical criteria
Economic criteria set cannot be satisfied	Before a project is accepted ensure that there is a reasonable chance that the economic criteria specified can be satisfied
Socio-political climate changes and makes project unacceptable	Before getting involved in a project determine that the socio-political climate of the project represents no unacceptable risk. For overseas projects it is possible that dramatic changes in government disrupt a project. It is possible to obtain insurance against such political disruption
Contractual arrangements introduce risks that cause contracts to fail	Before accepting a contract check that the risk implications are acceptable

Spectrum of risks to be considered

It is possible to envisage a near infinite spectrum of risks that should be considered before deciding whether or not to be involved in a project. Assessors of major projects often consider several hundred factors. It is not always possible to evaluate each factor in such a large range of factors with the same degree of accuracy. It is also possible that the range of factors considered misses, for some reason, a factor that turns out to be of critical importance. The reason for the omission may be inadequacy of the assessor's knowledge, or that the significance of the factor had not been recognised by anyone. Some of the important factors that should be considered are listed in Table 29.

The diversity of the factors in the list exposes the importance of finding some consistent way of rating the acceptability of the risk associated with every factor. At this point, attention is just drawn to the need for such a rating and the subject of rating is returned to in the next section, where the topic is the central issue examined.

Natural disasters can also be the cause of project failures. In recent years the cost of natural disasters as measured by insured losses has risen from about 0·2% of gross domestic product in the period 1970 to 1989 to about 0·4% of gross domestic product in the period after 1989.[56] In 1992 due to Hurricane Andrew losses reached 1·2% of gross domestic product (US$ 22·5 billion).[61] Clearly, all natural disaster losses are not related to project failures but certainly it is a factor that has to be considered in major construction projects. Two simple examples illustrate the significance of the factor.

(*a*)   Strong winds may make it impossible to tow an oil-rig platform into position for several weeks. Such a delay may cost the oil company millions of US$ in lost revenue.

(*b*)   Storms may make it unsafe to work on the completion of a bridge because it would not be possible to lift vital components into position. Also, the partially finished bridge may not be as strong as the finished bridge, therefore it may not be able to withstand the onset of storms.

Some projects may not be insured against all natural disaster losses. In such cases in the event of a disaster the proposers will have to make up the difference between insured cover and the real loss. If the proposer cannot fund the loss from his/her own resources or from the project's sponsors the project may just have to be abandoned.

Evaluation of risks

In Table 29, 55 risk factors are identified. The list is not comprehensive; in some cases more factors and in other cases fewer factors will need to be considered, but the table gives an indication of the range of factors that may be involved. In projects where government finance is involved the factors that have to be considered may include: the extent to which the project will help to preserve or develop a special range of capabilities; the need to collaborate with other governments;

Table 29. Essential factors that should be considered in the assessment of the acceptability of the risks in a major project

Risk	Assessment risk
Design	*Manufacture/construction*
Cost of redesign work required due to poor preliminary design	Unforeseen staff costs
Specification flawed	Safety problems
Substandard design requires modification	Risks of cost and time overrun
Risks that specification will change during design stage	Materials used cause unforeseen problems
	Under/over ordering of materials
Cost or time delay due to proving materials to be used	Unexpected toxicity problems
	Unexpected impact of legislation
Regulatory type delays such as planning permission delays	Environmental problems
	Completion to time and budget causes problems
Failure of design contractor or major sub-contractor	Changes in price and quantity of materials, labour and plant
Time and cost overruns	Contractor deviates from design
Non-compliance with specifications	Third party claims for damage, pollution loss or injury
Design fails audit	
Undetected design errors	
Other risks	*Operational*
Contractual complications	Business interruption
Unusual contract	Major accident
Delay due to legislation	Unexpected operational costs
Results of R& D show design should be changed	Third party claims
	Installation does not perform as expected
R&D does not cover all potential risks	Supplier performance inadequate
Inflation causes contractual problems	Equipment unreliable
Insolvency of promoter or financial supporter	
	Maintenance
Tax, VAT, capital allowances, etc., problems	
	Risk of unforeseen maintenance
Inability to refinance	Materials/labour price increase
Patent rights problems	Remedying unexpected defects
Riot, invasion, terrorism, etc.	Non-compliance with maintenance manuals or updates
Change of government or change of government policy	Inadequate maintenance due to inferior materials
Loss of lead staff	Maintenance processes take longer than expected
Strikes	
Force majeure	
Corruption	
Vandalism	
Natural disasters, including weather	

and the need to provide employment in a particular area. In real life the exact range of factors that have to be considered must be tailored to the precise nature of the project involved.

Regardless of the number of factors that have to be considered, a way must be found of rating the acceptability of the risk associated with each factor. Then when the risk acceptability of each factor has been determined, an acceptable way has to be found of integrating the risk acceptability of all the factors to give an overall rating of the acceptability of the project as a whole.

The evaluation of acceptability would be a relatively simple matter if each factor could be assessed in quantitative terms measured in the same units. In reality the determination of the risk associated with the whole range of factors will involve a complex array of units; some based on precise objective measurements in clearly defined units, other factors will be judged in subjective qualitative terms with a considerable degree of uncertainty associated with each judgement. In some cases, particularly with novel projects, there may initially be no hard evidence on which to base an assessment. In such cases where the only data are mainly subjective qualitative evidence, the assessment methods used have to be pragmatic. However, in attempting to identify the optimum solution, care must be taken to follow the best traditions of statistical analysis and to quantify the assessment as much as possible before major financial commitments are entered into. Assessing the level of risk associated with a proposed project and determining the acceptability of the risks both require recognition that some uncertainty is associated with every assessment.

Methodology for evaluation of project risk uncertainties
Without repeating the discussion on the significance of evaluating uncertainty in assessments given in chapter 4 and without trespassing too much on the discussion in chapter 9, there are some important features that have to be recognised about the process of evaluating risks. Although a range of risk acceptability determining factors is identified in Table 29, it sometimes gives a greater insight into their significance to consider them, at least initially, under the headings of technical and funding acceptability.

The heading *technical acceptability* is intended to cover satisfaction of all the technical criteria set for the various parts of a project. The overall technical acceptability criteria may be something like an engine that has to produce a certain power output for a particular level of fuel consumption or a chemical plant that has to produce a certain level of product output without causing any environmentally unfriendly products to be generated. These are just two simple examples of the enormous range of technical criteria that may be involved.

Funding acceptability is an equally broad heading and is intended to cover determination of the adequacy of funding to satisfy all contingencies in the life of a project. The funding of major projects is rarely a simple matter, often finance is arranged through a consortium of banks or other financial institutions. Although the institutions use the consortium approach as a way of reducing their risk exposure, the diversity of lenders can introduce problems for borrowers. The problems may include slower decision-making and different lenders having different requirements.

Another type of project finance that is being tried, particularly for major projects in which the government has an interest, is Private Finance Initiative (PFI). The justification for adopting PFI is the view that private sector management can deliver substantial savings on public sector projects, although it is appreciated that PFI is not universally applicable.[62] Typically, in a PFI project, a consortium of private companies undertake to design, build and operate a particular service/project and recover the cost of its investment from the fee it is paid for operating the service/project throughout its life.

The risks taken by the private sector are to some extent limited by the contract it accepts from the public sector. To describe these risks simply as the risks associated with any contractual arrangement is a misleading over-simplification. The private sector provides the funding at the beginning of the project and earns its return on its investment in the form of a rent paid by the public sector throughout the life of the project. The risks retained by the private sector include non-recoverable errors in costing, failure of the project, cancellation of the project, and failure and inadequacies of members of the consortium.

There is also another type of risk that potential participants in PFI projects have to consider, which is that their tender may not win. Generally, PFI projects have to be tendered for and the cost of preparing a tender is quite high. So if a company's tender is not successful the cost of preparing a tender becomes a loss. Because the cost of preparing tenders is so high, only fairly large companies have adequate financial resources.

In PFI projects the public sector cannot divest itself of all risk. The residual public sector risks include continued demand for the project; the design of the project becoming obsolete; failure of the project and

Table 30. An outline of project contingencies that might give rise to project funding problems

Contingency	Nature of impact on funding
Client has cash flow/budget problems	Project might be delayed or slowed down — late payments might give contractors problems
Additional construction work has to be done	Client may take time to find additional funding required
Design weaknesses found	Delays project and increases cost
Additional research and development required	Delays project, may cause redesign and increases cost
Satisfying safety regulations	Delays completion and handover of project. Delays revenue earning and increases cost.
Public and government opinion turns against project	Project may be stopped or delayed, increases overall cost or even loss of all money spent if project stopped
Government gets into financial problems and cannot pay for work done	Some kind of insurance may be required to cover such an event
Contractors go bankrupt	Project delayed while new contractors found, costs increased
Novel contractual requirements prove to be more expensive to satisfy than anticipated at the time the contract was signed	Contractor has to find extra financing which may overstress the contractor's financial resources

changes in legislation. PFI projects are also likely to be sensitive to changes in government policy.

One important conclusion from this very brief review of PFI type projects is that all parties must understand the range and nature of the risks involved and the implications of the way they are allocated.

There are many contingencies that may need funding, an outline of the different types of contingency that might give rise to funding problems is shown in Table 30. Beside assessing the contingencies that have to be allowed for, the decision-maker has to decide which of the options open will yield the greatest benefit for the funds invested. One method is to calculate the present value on the basis of the discounted cash which is: present value = the sum of all the cash flows/discount rate. The discount rate being the interest rate required plus an adjustment factor to allow for the risk involved. The adjustment factor could be considered as a risk premium. It seems likely that the discounted cash flow approach is likely to be replaced by the Adjusted Present Value (APV) or Equity Cash Flow (ECF) approaches.[63, 64] The merit claimed for ECF is that in calculating the benefit of the cash flows to equity it used a discount rate that compensates for the risk being borne.

Our reason for drawing attention to the use of various methods of cash flow calculation is to show how obvious the sources of uncertainty are in estimating benefit. All the discounted cash flow methods depend on predictions of cash flow. Predictions of future outcomes are always subject to some uncertainty.

Public opinion turning against the project is included as a contingency; this is just one aspect of the spectrum of socio-political factors that may influence the acceptability of a project. Public protesters may delay a project and increase costs and delay completion. A change of government might result in the project being stopped. A government might get into financial trouble and be unable to pay for work already done. The nature and influence of socio-political factors are considered further in chapters 9 and 10.

6

Medical risks

In this chapter a very broad definition of the word medical *is used. The word is taken to include all causes of death and the action taken to lessen the impact of such causes. The aim of the chapter is to identify the significance of the various components of the spectrum of media risks that are an intrinsic part of all our lives. The argument presented is divided into five parts: the pattern of causes of death; efficacy requirements for pharmaceuticals, the risk implications of constraints on medical treatment expenditure; public influence on the reduction of medical risks; and conclusions that appear to be justified.*

Pattern of causes of death

There are considerable differences between countries in the level of medical risks to which their populations are exposed. The consequence of these differences is illustrated by the variation in life expectancy. Table 31 shows something of the current range of life expectancy. In assessing the consequences of exposure to hazardous conditions, it must be remembered that not all people exposed to harmful conditions experience the same harmful effects. For example, only a proportion of a group of people similarly exposed to lung toxicity or carcinogenic conditions suffer harmful effects.[65] No attempt is made in this book to explain why there are differences in the way people react to exposure to toxic conditions.

In the World Health Organisation's (WHO) annual statistics, a methodology has been adopted that classifies cause of death under one of a hundred and two possible causes.[66] These causes can be considered as being the main causes of death and they are listed in Table 32.

Table 31. Life expectancy for a sample of countries

Country	Life expectancy Males	Life expectancy Females
United States of America	69	77
China	60	63
Russia	64	74
United Kingdom	68	74
Sweden	72	78
Kenya	47	51
India	42	41
Australia	68	74
Argentina	65	71

There are considerable differences in the nature of the various potential causes of death. Also, there are large differences in the incidence of the various causes of death. In the United Kingdom, just over 47% of the causes give rise to more than 1000 deaths per 100 000 people. The distribution of cause of death rate varies between countries and with age and sex.

Tables 33 to 37 show, drawing on WHO data, how for a sample of countries the incidence of some causes of death has changed over the years 1950 to 1989.[66] The main criteria that determined the selection of the countries in the sample was availability of comparable data.

This resulted in the five countries examined having standards of living within a fairly narrow range of about four to one. It should be noted that the tables do not identify, for the countries considered, differences in the conditions the people were exposed to that would result in death due to particular causes.

The main conclusions suggested by the data for the period 1950–1989 given in Tables 33 to 37 are as follows.

- Tuberculosis seemed to be falling as a cause of death in all countries considered.
- In Argentina, malignant neoplasm as a cause of death seemed to be falling, but in the other four countries considered, malignant neoplasms seem to be increasing as a cause of death.
- Diabetes as a cause of death seemed to be fairly constant but it is about 40% higher in Argentina than the other countries.
- Diseases of the circulatory system are the major cause of death, but its incidence as the cause of death seems to have been falling over the period considered.

- Respiratory diseases as a cause of death increased except in the UK and Australia where there was a slight downward trend.
- There was a reduction of deaths due to injury and poisoning.
- There was a reduction in the number of deaths attributed to motor vehicle traffic accidents.
- Suicide and self-inflicted injury as a cause of death remained more or less at the same level.
- For the causes of death considered the number of women dying of the causes identified is less than the number of men dying of the same cause, but the tables do not include conditions such as childbirth or breast cancer that are unique to women.

In Tables 33 to 37 deaths due to injury or poisoning have been grouped together; other figures in ref. 66 show that deaths due to drugs or medicaments causing adverse therapeutic effect have an incidence about a quarter of that of injury and poisoning. That is of the order of 10 per 100 000 deaths. For comparison, Table 38 lists the more common risks of death we all face. The figures suggest that public concern increases when the risk of an activity increase to significantly more than 1 in 100 000 per year. Specifically, in the medical field, public concern is expressed when prophylactic treatments, such as vaccination of children against measles, mumps and rubella, show serious side effects at a level of 7 in 100 000.[67] This concern also illustrates how the acceptability of risk varies with the circumstances. Concern to limit risks to children perhaps being higher than some other kinds of risk.

Some additional insights into the cause of death are given by the deaths reported to coroners.[68] The deaths reported to coroners are those where the doctor in attendance at or after death did not have sufficient information about the medical history of the deceased to be able to write a medical certificate showing the cause of death. In England and Wales about a third of all deaths are reported to coroners; in about 12% of these cases inquests are held. Table 39 summarises the distribution of verdicts in 1995 and shows that accidental deaths and suicides were the most common causes of death recorded. The figures are not directly comparable with the figures in Tables 33 to 38 which are for the whole population of the countries considered. However, the figures do indicate that there may be some sections of the population more at risk than other sections.

The impression should not be given that patterns of diseases are constant. New viruses are constantly being exposed and these represent one of the biggest threats to mankind. In the past 20 years scientists have discovered about 30 new diseases.[70] Most of these have been spread

Table 32 (below and facing). List of the causes of death adopted in WHO statistics

Infectious and parasitic diseases	Malignant neoplasm of cervix uteri	Diseases of pulmonary circulation and other forms of heart disorder	All other indirect obstetric causes
Typhoid fever	Malignant neoplasm of uterus, other and unspecified	Cerebrovascular disease	Diseases of skin and subcutaneous tissue
Other intestinal infectious diseases	Malignant neoplasm of prostate	Atherosclerosis	Diseases of the musculoskeletal system and connective tissue
Tuberculosis of respiratory system	Malignant neoplasm of bladder	Embolism, thrombosis and other diseases of the arteries	Spina bifida and hydrocephalus
Tuberculosis, other forms	Malignant neoplasm of other sites	Phlebitis, thrombophlebitis, venous embolism and thrombosis	Congenital anomalies of heart and circulatory system
Whooping cough	Leukaemia	Other diseases of the circulatory system	Other congenital anomalies
Meningococcal infection	Other malignant neoplasm of lymphatic and haemopoietic tissues	Acute upper respiratory infection	Birth trauma
Tetanus	Benign neoplasm, other and unspecified neoplasm	Acute bronchitis and bronchiolitis	Other conditions originating in the perinatal period
Septicaemia	Diabetes mellitus	Pneumonia	Senility without mention of psychosis
Other bacterial diseases	Other endocrine and metabolic diseases	Influenza	Signs, symptoms and other ill-defined conditions
Measles	Nutritional marasmus	Bronchitis, chronic and unspecified, emphysema and asthma	Accidents and adverse effects
Other viral diseases	Other protein-calorie malnutrition	Other diseases of the respiratory system	Motor vehicle traffic accidents

Table 32 — continued

Malaria	Other nutritional deficiencies	Ulcer of stomach and duodenum	Other transport accidents
Other arthropod-borne diseases	Anaemia	Appendicitis	Accidental poisoning
Venereal diseases	Other diseases of blood and blood-forming organs	Hernia of abdominal cavity and intestinal obstruction	Accidental falls
Other infectious and parasitic diseases	Mental disorders	Chronic liver disease and cirrhosis	Accidents caused by fire and flames
Malignant neoplasm	Meningitis	Other diseases of the digestive system	Accidental drowning and submersion
Malignant neoplasm of lip, oral cavity and pharynx	Multiple sclerosis	Nephritis, nephrotic syndrome and nephrosis	Accidents caused by machinery and piercing instruments
Malignant neoplasm of oesophagus	Epilepsy	Infections of kidney	Accidents caused by firearm missile
Malignant neoplasm of stomach	Other diseases of the nervous system	Hyperplasia of prostate	All other accidents including late effects
Malignant neoplasm of colon	Diseases of the circulatory system	Other diseases of the genitourinary system	Drugs, medicaments causing adverse effects in therapeutic use
Malignant neoplasm of rectum, rectosigmoid junction and anus	Acute rheumatic fever	Abortion	Suicide and self-inflicted injury
Malignant neoplasm of liver, spc. as primary	Chronic rheumatic heart disease	Haemorrhage of pregnancy and childbirth	Homicide and injury purposely inflicted by other persons
Malignant neoplasm of larynx	Hypersensitive disease	Toxaemia of pregnancy	Other violence
Malignant neoplasm of trachea	Acute myocardial infection	Complications of the puerperium	
Malignant neoplasm of female breast	Other chronic heart diseases	Other direct obstetric causes	

Table 33. Changes in the cause of death over the period 1950–1989 for the United States of America

Disease	Age standardised death rate per 100 000 people							
	1950–54	1955–59	1960–64	1965–69	1970–74	1975–79	1980–84	1985–89
Tuberculosis								
Men	27	15	11	7	4	3	2	1
Women	12	5	3	2	1	1	1	1
Malignant neoplasms								
Men	222	231	240	253	266	274	282	283
Women	185	177	171	170	169	169	174	178
Diabetes								
Men	19	19	21	23	23	19	18	19
Women	28	25	26	26	25	19	18	18
Diseases of the circulatory system								
Men	952	950	949	918	860	726	644	560
Women	699	677	653	615	545	444	398	357
Diseases of the respiratory system								
Men	70	78	95	108	108	102	106	116
Women	44	43	48	49	44	41	46	59
Injury and poisoning								
Men	103	120	116	128	128	113	102	95
Women	57	50	48	51	48	40	35	33
Motor vehicle traffic accidents								
Men	41	39	38	44	46	33	30	28
Women	12	12	13	15	14	12	11	11
Suicide and self-inflicted injury								
Men	20	20	21	20	21	21	21	22
Women	5	5	6	7	7	7	6	5

Table 34. Changes in the cause of death over the period 1950–1989 for the United Kingdom

Disease	Age standardised death rate per 100 000 people							
	1950–54	1955–59	1960–64	1965–69	1970–74	1975–79	1980–84	1985–89
Tuberculosis								
Men	38	18	12	8	5	3	2	1
Women	19	7	4	2	2	1	1	1
Malignant neoplasms								
Men	274	289	301	317	324	329	327	329
Women	191	187	186	187	193	199	202	210
Diabetes								
Men	8	7	8	10	11	11	11	15
Women	11	10	10	11	11	10	9	12
Diseases of the circulatory system								
Men	933	908	901	877	850	801	712	631
Women	710	670	637	585	651	506	439	390
Diseases of the respiratory system								
Men	231	235	258	270	272	267	226	166
Women	127	113	117	121	127	134	118	85
Injury and poisoning								
Men	69	73	73	67	62	59	54	50
Women	38	41	43	40	38	35	29	24
Motor vehicle traffic accidents								
Men	17	20	23	23	22	19	15	14
Women	5	6	8	8	8	7	6	5
Suicide and self-inflicted injury								
Men	15	15	15	13	10	11	12	12
Women	7	8	9	8	6	6	6	5

Table 35. Changes in the cause of death over the period 1950–1989 for Sweden

Disease	Age standardised death rate per 100 000 people							
	1950–54	1955–59	1960–64	1965–69	1970–74	1975–79	1980–84	1985–89
Tuberculosis								
Men	23	12	9	7	7	5	3	1
Women	14	7	4	3	3	2	1	1
Malignant neoplasms								
Men	202	213	231	230	258	271	243	236
Women	183	182	182	175	187	185	171	164
Diabetes								
Men	11	11	15	18	15	16	14	15
Women	16	14	18	20	15	15	12	12
Diseases of the circulatory system								
Men	702	722	732	717	710	702	679	610
Women	640	622	585	531	473	434	403	357
Diseases of the respiratory system								
Men	81	85	86	103	68	78	89	95
Women	73	73	68	74	41	43	48	52
Injury and poisoning								
Men	92	94	95	96	101	100	84	79
Women	40	40	45	43	48	49	37	34
Motor vehicle traffic accidents								
Men	21	22	25	25	23	19	14	14
Women	5	6	8	9	9	8	6	6
Suicide and self-inflicted injury								
Men	28	30	28	31	30	28	27	26
Women	8	9	9	11	12	12	11	10

Table 36. Changes in the cause of death over the period 1950–1989 for Australia

Disease	Age standardised death rate per 100 000 people							
	1950–54	1955–59	1960–64	1965–69	1970–74	1975–79	1980–84	1985–89
Tuberculosis								
Men	28	14	10	6	3	2	1	1
Women	9	4	2	1	1	1	0	0
Malignant neoplasms								
Men	218	229	238	256	278	281	290	292
Women	170	165	161	160	168	163	166	169
Diabetes								
Men	15	15	18	22	23	20	18	18
Women	24	22	21	23	22	16	15	14
Diseases of the circulatory system								
Men	941	942	963	992	962	796	674	565
Women	706	678	663	661	638	519	433	373
Diseases of the respiratory system								
Men	125	137	141	159	166	140	127	116
Women	72	67	57	57	55	47	44	46
Injury and poisoning								
Men	119	116	112	113	110	81	35	28
Women	50	51	51	55	51	43	33	30
Motor vehicle traffic accidents								
Men	42	43	44	47	46	40	31	26
Women	10	11	14	16	16	15	12	10
Suicide and self-inflicted injury								
Men	18	20	22	22	20	18	19	21
Women	6	7	10	11	9	7	6	6

Table 37. Changes in the cause of death over the period 1950–1989 for Argentina

Disease	Age standardised death rate per 100 000 people							
	1950–54	1955–59	1960–64	1965–69	1970–74	1975–79	1980–84	1985–89
Tuberculosis								
Men			N/A		22	13	10	8
Women					11	6	4	3
Malignant neoplasms								
Men			N/A		307	272	250	260
Women					192	174	160	162
Diabetes								
Men			N/A		34	29	26	28
Women					36	28	25	25
Diseases of the circulatory system								
Men			N/A		746	766	751	705
Women					518	562	549	502
Diseases of the respiratory system								
Men			N/A		93	89	98	104
Women					57	51	53	56
Injury and poisoning								
Men			N/A		110	107	92	92
Women					37	38	35	34
Motor vehicle traffic accidents								
Men			N/A		29	25	20	17
Women					8	8	6	5
Suicide and self-inflicted injury								
Men			N/A		18	14	13	14
Women					5	4	4	5

Table 38. Some common risks of death

Cause	Risk of dying in one year
All natural causes at the age of 40	1 in 850
Accident at home	1 in 26 000
Accident at work (This is an average figure for all types of work. Some types of work have a higher risk and others have a lower risk)	1 in 45 000 (2·2 in 100 000)
Being hit by lightning	1 in 1 000 000

Table 39. Verdicts returned at inquests, 1995

Verdict	Males	Females	Total	Number per 100 000 registered deaths
Homicide, of which:				
killed unlawfully	123	94	217	38
killed lawfully	3	3	6	1
Suicide	2829	750	3579	632
Attempted or self-induced abortion	0	0	0	0
Cause of death aggravated by lack of care or self neglect	16	19	35	6
Dependence on drugs	115	24	139	25
Non-dependent abuse of drugs	142	20	162	29
Want of attention at birth	8	1	9	2
Death from industrial diseases*	1792	86	1878	332
Death by accident or misadventure	5780	3362	9142	1615
Stillborn	6	2	8	1
Deaths from natural causes	1625	858	2483	439
Open verdicts	1523	734	2257	399
All other verdicts	85	51	136	24
Total	14 047	6004	20 051	3543

* It has been suggested that in the United Kingdom the overall cost to society of work related accidents and ill health represents between 1 and 2% of the country's Gross Domestic Product (GDP).[69](In chapter 8 this cost is compared with the cost of lost working time due to sports injuries.)

from animals to man. All are immune to antibiotics, and they can mutate so fast that the handful of antiviral drugs available quickly become obsolete. An example of how fast viruses travel is given by HIV. Thirty years ago HIV was unknown in humans, now it is present on every continent and affects 23 million people! Exposure and spread of viruses is facilitated, to some extent, by changing ecological systems and fast global travel.

Other dramatic changes in the pattern of disease are

- between 1973 and 1991 there was a 126% increase in prostate cancer
- between 1961 and 1991 there was a 96% increase in lung cancer deaths among men and a staggering 451% increase among women.[71]

It is also important to note that the pattern of exposure to substances that may be detrimental to health changes with time. Also, the understanding of the way different potentially harmful substances may harm health is not completely understood.[72] Recently, an international working group was convened to develop a conceptual framework for the assessment of the risks of human disease associated with pathogenic micro-organisms. The behaviour of micro-organisms in the human body is quite different from that of chemicals; micro-organisms have the ability to survive and to multiply in the body in which they find themselves.

The effect on health of exposure to any potentially harmful substance or organism depends on three interactive factors, namely

(a) host characteristics
(b) nature of the health effects
(c) the dose–response relationship.

The host characteristics include the health, age and living environment of those exposed. The health effects include whether the exposure is likely to be fatal or to lead to the development of some condition that is recoverable. The whole spectrum of dose–response relationship may be very difficult to establish with precision. For new substances or organisms only part of the dose–response relationship may be known.

Efficacy requirements for pharmaceuticals

The efficacy of pharmaceuticals, like most medical procedures, is amenable to risk assessment. The general question of medical risk assessment is discussed further in appendix 3. In most developed countries there are fairly strict regulations about the way the efficacy of pharmaceuticals has to be tested before they are allowed to be put on the market.

There are some international requirements and, in some cases, national requirements are slightly different. In the countries of the European Community there are a series of directives that set out the protocols and procedures that should be followed in determination of the acceptability of pharmaceutical products.[73, 74]

For a pharmaceutical product to be accepted for marketing, it has to be shown that

- the substance is efficacious or at least that it has no unacceptable side effects
- the substance as produced for the market includes nothing that would make it unacceptable
- the substance does not cause any adverse conditions, if this has been proven by long-term monitoring.

Proving that the long-term and short-term efficacy of a pharmaceutical product is acceptable is not a simple matter. There is an element of uncertainty at each stage. In Table 40 a summary is given of the experimental procedures that may be involved and the type of uncertainty that may be associated with the results.

When all the evidence is obtained, the investigation will be expected to express an opinion on the acceptability of the product, taking into account its compatibility, its therapeutic efficacy and any contraindications in normal use. It is important that abnormal use is excluded because that would need experimental work to determine just how efficacious the product was under the precise abnormal conditions.

The experimentally obtained evidence about the behaviour of a pharmaceutical product is not the total measure of the uncertainty associated with its efficacy. The product may not be prescribed at an appropriate time; the product may not be taken at the appropriate dosage and dose rate. In a slightly different way the patient may not receive the product because insufficient funds are available for its purchase. There may also be arguments that the patient is in a permanent deep coma and is only kept alive by a machine so it is not worth giving the medication. Some of these issues raise very deep medical ethical arguments, which are a little to one side of the arguments in this book.

Risk implications of constraints on expenditure on medical treatment

In the context of what is an acceptable risk, it is interesting to note that it has been suggested by the UK Government's Chief Medical Officer

85

Table 40. A summary of experimental procedures that may be used in determining the efficacy of a pharmaceutical product

Test	Nature of uncertainty	Comments
Toxic reaction — test on two mammalian species	Species on which tests were made may not respond in exactly the same way as humans and test may only be of short duration	There should be enough evidence obtained to enable a rigorous statistical analysis to be made
Repeated dose toxicity	The test period may still be too short to ensure all adverse responses are detected	There should be enough evidence obtained to enable a rigorous statistical analysis to be made
Teratogenic effects (causing malformation of an embryo)	May be difficult to confirm that the product being tested is the real cause of teratogenic effects*	It is important that the reaction to the product is tested on the full range of people it may be used on
Reaction when the new product is used in combination with other matters	Adequacy in statistical terms of dose effect and time effect experiments	There should be enough evidence to enable a rigorous statistical analysis to be made of the efficacy of the product
Fate of substance with the organism	All organisms involved may not be identified	How does the substance really react
Clinical trials on particular groups	There may be groups (such as older or younger people) who may react differently to the substance	The group used for clinical trials may have people in it with several diseases which will complicate interpretation of the results

* Some of the teratogenic effects of chemicals were mentioned in chapter 5.

that, in the future, surgical procedures and medical drugs should carry a risk rating to help patients assess the chance of anything going wrong.[75, 76] The points on the risk scale as recognised by the Chief Medical Officer are shown in Table 41. Negligible risks are shown to be those where the risk of dying in one year is one in a million, while high risks are those where the risk of dying in a year is one in a hundred or higher. For comparison the risk of being killed by lightning is one in a million. It is a very important step forward that some parts of the medical

Table 41. Risk of dying in any one year or developing an adverse response

Action	Risk
Transmission to susceptible household contacts of measles and chickenpox (A)*	High
Transmission of HIV from mother to child (Europe) (A)	greater than 1:100
Gastro-intestinal effects of antibiotics (A)	
Smoking ten cigarettes per day (D)	Moderate
All natural causes, age 40 years (D)	1:100–1:1000
All kinds of violence and poisoning (D)	Low
Influenza (D)	1:1000–1:10 000
Accident on road (D)	
Leukaemia (D)	
Playing soccer (D)	Very low
Accident at home (D)	1:10 000–1:100 000
Accident at work (D)	
Homicide (D)	
Accident on railway (D)	Minimal
Vaccination-associated polio (A)	1:100 000–1:1 000 000
Hit by lightning (D)	Negligible
Release of radiation by nuclear power station (D)	lower than 1:1 000 000

* In the table, (D) is the risk of dying and (A) is the risk of adverse response.

profession consider that they can discuss with their patients the risks associated with medical procedures in quantitative terms. There will, of course, be cases where because the patient has no understanding of information expressed in quantitative terms, it would be inappropriate to discuss the risk in such terms. However, quantitative knowledge of risks does give confidence that a precise understandable qualitative comparison of risk can be presented to patients. Most would recognise that a risk equal to that of being struck by lightning is a negligible risk.

There is, as with all forms of expenditure, a finite limit to what can be spent on medical treatments. Besides a finite limit on overall expenditure there is a tremendous variation between people and the amount they are able to spend on medical care. If a state undertakes to provide a medical service to all there will be some level of service fixed by government budget constraints. The poor will have to accept the level of service fixed by budget constraints, and the rich will be able to buy some additional medical services which in medical terms may improve both their quality of life and their life expectancy.

In hard, realistic terms this means that state budgeting controls place a limit on the life expectancy of some people and the quality of life they may enjoy. This budgetary limit is normally described in money terms, but it could be described as specifying the level of health risk that people in general will have to accept. The risk may be reducing life expectancy or leaving some conditions untreated.

State budgeting and private resources are not the only constraints determining how much medical treatment can be bought. Firms that own the patent on a medical drug are usually allowed to charge more than they would be able to were they operating in a truly competitive market.[77]

Another way of looking at the concern about reducing the risk associated with medical treatments is the amount of money that is allocated to medical research. In 1995–96 the European Commission allocated 140 million ECU (about £100 million) to medical research projects.[78] Generally, the European Commission funds research on a shared cost basis, so the total amount spent on the range of projects it funds will be in excess of £200 million. The money the European Commission spends is a small part of the total expenditure on medical research. Many pharmaceutical firms have their own massive research programmes and prefer to keep them confidential until the results are proven to be successful and are covered by patents.

Public influence on the reduction of medical risks

It has been argued by one eminent American medical doctor that people are often wary, even fearful, of new technologies.[79] Some apprehension is simply fear of the unknown and can be overcome, but the emotional dimension of the public's concern about technology's potential risk and threats to itself or the environment is less readily addressed. This factor can have a profound impact on consumers' acceptance of new technology, as well as on public policies affecting technology.

As governments make decisions about consumer products, fear and intimidation from several possible sources may distort the accurate assessment of risks, benefits and possible alternatives. This can lead to decisions that are, in the long-term, harmful from both an economic and humanitarian perspective. Understanding the emotional dimensions can help governments to make more clearheaded decisions and to remain free from cynical manipulation. Several factors can cloud thinking about risks. Two factors of particular importance are as follows.

(a)   *Uncertainty and ambiguity.* Studies of risk perception have shown that people tend to overestimate risks that are unfamiliar, hard to understand, invisible, involuntary or potentially catastrophic. Thus, invisible threats such as electromagnetic radiation or trace amounts of pesticides in food can inspire uncertainty and fear. A contributory factor to this response may be poor scientific literacy in general and unfamiliarity with the statistical aspects of risk in particular.

   Genetically engineered vaccines and antibiotics are examples of products that in some quarters have been viewed with suspicion. Those people that develop fear or suspicion often fail to take into account the risks of the alternative of not using the genetically manufactured substances.

(b)   *Information overload.* This can be a problem with non-experts who only understand a limited number of aspects of a risk analysis problem, and easily become overloaded with data. Information overload of the public is a strategy used by those who would disparage or promote fear about new technology. Anti-biotechnology activists may deluge the public with irrelevant, inaccurate, or (just as harmful) partly true information that leaves the non-expert bewildered. Overabundant information may encourage some people who are interested in the subject to focus on unusual and dramatic aspects of the problem instead of on representative valid data and statistics.

   Consumers should exercise their right to have and to choose among new products in the market-place, subject to rational and sensible government regulation that eschews condescension and misinformation. Another aspect of this problem is that people may choose to ignore sound advice not only in respect of new technologies but also in relation to what they consider as their natural surroundings. Protection against exposure to ultraviolet light and the risk of developing skin cancer is something that many outdoor workers prefer to ignore. In the Netherlands, where about 20 000 new cases of skin cancer are reported per year (that is 1 in every 7500 of the population), a survey showed that half the outdoor workers questioned said that they did not bother with protection against ultraviolet light. [80]

   While fears of the risks associated with new technologies, or perhaps more generally just unfamiliar situations, may be inevitable, they can and should be tempered with knowledge. In this context it is worth remembering Sherlock Holmes' admonition in *Scandal in Bohemia* that 'it is a capital mistake to theorise before one has data'.

The question of what budget constraints mean in terms of medical treatments is such a contentious issue that politicians prefer to camouflage the discussion by using terms such as *rationing* and *setting priorities* without making clear the implications of the discussion.[75] The hidden assumption seems to be that, because of the complex nature of the medical issues involved, the public would not understand the argument. The moral obligation for the politicians involved in policy-making to put the arguments in understandable terms and to seek public approval appears to be ignored. The discussion is clouded further by medical professionals relying on ill-defined terms such as *medical ethics* or *clinical evidence* to support their views.

The essential feature of the debate should be that if it concerns the public and services that they pay for through taxes, the debate should be conducted in a way that is transparent to all interested parties. Interested parties are not only those participating in the discussion but also those who may be affected by the outcome of the debate. It may mean that the debate has to be conducted in terms of the maximum amount that can be spent on a patient or the probability that a treatment will be successful. A successful treatment would have to be defined, perhaps in terms of extending life by at least a year, or improving the quality of the patient's life in some demonstrable way. If treatment has to be denied there is a moral obligation, backed by professional obligations derived from the Hippocratic Oath, that the patient must be left comfortable. One version of the oath is given in appendix 4. The sentence in the oath that encapsulates the medical approach to risk states

> *The regimen I adopt shall be for the benefit of my patients according to my ability and judgement, and not for their hurt or for any wrong.*

Conclusions

In many ways the medical field represents a complete system of risk evaluation, risk acceptance and risk communication. The medical doctor has to diagnose the patient's condition and then to decide on the action to be taken that is most likely to be successful, whereupon the situation has to be explained to the patient. Only occasionally will it be possible or appropriate to make the explanation of the risk involved in quantitative terms. The system is not static, it is constantly changing; patterns of diseases are changing; the range of treatments available is always changing; and exposure to hazards change.

The UK Government Chief Medical Officer's classification of the acceptability of risks gives a good indication of the rating of risks in the medical field. He suggested that a negligible risk is the chance of someone dying in one year of one in a million, and high risks are those where the risk of dying in a year is one in a hundred or higher.[81]

The risks associated with particular medical treatments or procedures and their acceptability when related to the patient's condition illustrate well how the level of acceptable risk can vary with circumstances.

7

Transport risks

This chapter examines the nature of the risks in road, rail, air and sea transport, and attempts to compare the incidence of accidents on an international basis. From the data examined, an attempt is made to identify the features that are common to all transport risks and the optimum method of assessing the significance of those risks.

Humans always seem to have had an inclination to travel. Perhaps at first the inclination was satisfied by walking and swinging from trees. Then came the interest in riding on animals and travelling on water. At present we still walk a little but travel many miles by car, bus, train, ship and aeroplane. Some people have even journeyed as far as the moon. To put transport risks into perspective, some essential statistics are given in this chapter. An assessment of the significance of the evidence is then given which includes an attempt to identify the optimum method of assessing the significance of transport risks. Some important dates in the development of transport are reported in appendix 5.

In order to put the essential statistics on an international basis the data from three countries are considered. The three countries are Britain, France and USA. Table 42 gives the general statistics of the countries describing their size and gross domestic product. Of the countries considered, the USA has the highest gross domestic product per head of population; it is 60% higher than Britain's, which of the three considered has the lowest gross domestic product per head of population. The density of population per square kilometre is roughly nine times higher in Britain than in the USA.

Four forms of transport are considered, namely road, rail, air and sea.

Table 42. General statistics of the countries considered*

Country	Population in millions	Area in thousands of km^2	Population per km^2	Gross Domestic Product per head of population in £
Britain	56·6	230	246	10 792
France	57·5	552	104	14 512
USA	257·6	9373	27	16 209

* These figures are drawn from The Department of Transport's Transport Statistics Great Britain 1995 edition.[82]

Road

Looking first at road traffic, Table 43 compares the road traffic and road deaths in the three countries considered in Table 42. The tables only give a snapshot of road accidents in one year for a very small group of countries but allows comparison with some factors that may influence accident rates. The factors considered do not represent the whole portfolio of factors that influence the incidence of road accidents. Accidents may take other forms: they may be due to failure of a single component or of a whole system. For example, failure of the ship-to-shore bridge by which vehicles are loaded on a ship may cause the loss of vehicles, as happened recently in Calais.[84] Among the factors that are not considered in this study, but which may be important contributory factors, are: technical condition of vehicle; state of the roads; driving skill; condition of the driver; speed limits; and driving conditions. Perhaps there are

Table 43. Comparison of road traffic and road deaths in three countries*

Country	Roads thousands of kilometres	Roads per thousand km^2	Thousands of vehicles (including cars, trucks, motor cycles and buses)	Rate of death per 100 000 population	Car user death per billion car kilometres
Britain	364	1585	24 712	7	5
France	916	1675	30 740	17	not known
USA	6278	670	218 214	16	9

* These figures are drawn from The Department of Transport's Transport Statistics Great Britain 1995 edition[83] and cover a different period to those quoted in Tables 31 and 32.

Table 44. Distribution of accident severity in a typical area of Britain, 1994

	Pedes-trians	Pedal cycles	Powered two-wheelers	Public service vehicles	Car	Goods vehicles	Other vehicles
Fatal	10	3	4	41	0	1	1
Serious	148	61	135	499	6	33	3
Slight	368	346	316	3640	63	175	9
Total	526	410	455	4180	69	209	13
Percentage of all road accidents	9%	7%	7·75%	71·50%	1%	3·50%	0·25%

even differences between countries in their philosophy of acceptable risk.

Looking at road accidents in particular, the total number of accidents consists of four main groups of casualties, namely car occupant, pedestrian, motor cyclist and pedal cyclist. The incidence of accidents varies both with time and location.[85] The variation with time between different parts of England is quite startling: for example, between 1994 and the mean casualty rate for 1981–85 the casualty rate in Avon fell by 30% and in Greater London by 15%. By contrast, in Merseyside the rate increased by 40% and in Greater Manchester by 20%. In Great Britain in 1994 the total number of road casualties per million of the population was 5616; the number of slight casualties was 4720; the number of serious casualties was 831; and the number of fatal casualties was 65. This means that serious and fatal casualties made up 16% of the total. Table 44 shows how the incidence of accidents of various severity is distributed

Table 45. Accidental fatality rates for passenger travel in UK[87]

	Fatalities per 100 million	
Passenger travel by	*Hours*	*Km*
Bus or coach	0·1	0·04
Rail	4·8	0·1
Water	12	0·6
Air	15	0·03
Car	15	0·4
Foot	20	5·3
Pedal cycle	60	4·3
Two-wheeled motor vehicle	300	9·7

between various types of road user in a typical area of Britain with a population of one million. Other data compare the risk of various forms of road travel on the basis of the distance travelled. The figures are given in Table 45 and show that per kilometre travelled pedestrians, pedal cyclists and travellers by two-wheeled motor vehicles (motor scooters and motor cycles) are more at risk than travellers by car. This makes official encouragement of people to walk or travel by bike a little questionable! The figures do expose a very important statistical point, i.e. the units in which comparisons of risks are made has a major influence on the indicated relative importance of the risk. Simply considering the data in Table 45 shows that if a comparison is made on the basis of hours travelled using particular forms of transport, quite different conclusions are drawn than if the comparison is made on the basis of kilometres travelled. Other work shows that if the risk is measured in terms of the number of trips made, the ordering of the magnitude of risk of the different forms of transport is different from that obtained using either hours or kilometres travelled.[86]

Rail

Table 46 shows the casualty rate associated with travel on British Railways in the period 1990–1995. The figures exclude accidents involving trespassers, suicides and attempted suicides. Direct comparison of the figures for the average fatal accident rate associated with rail travel with that associated with road transport is difficult, as road accidents are quoted either as total accidents/year, or accidents per million people/ year, whereas rail accidents are often quoted per passenger mile. This problem of comparison is returned to in several places and later an attempt is made to put the comparison on a consistent basis.

A comparison between road deaths (Table 43) and rail deaths (Table 46) shows that for travelling the same distance the risk of being killed on the railways is about a quarter of the risk of being killed on the roads in Britain. If the risk is so much higher on the roads, why does anybody travel by car? Most of the reasons are likely to be associated with convenience. For example, most people travelling into London travel by some form of public transport, mainly because of the congested roads and poor parking facilities; many other places are not so easy to reach by public transport. Overall, people travel 18 times further by car than they do by rail. The car has the advantage that it is instantly available. By contrast, travel by train has to be at times determined by the railway company. In reality, the people of Britain travel in total about 648 billion kilometres per year by road and 35 billion kilometres

Table 46. The casualty rate in Britain associated with rail transport in the period 1990–95[88]

Type of injury	1990/91	1991/92	1992/93	1993/94	1994/95	Average over the period per billion passenger/ km
Deaths	35	30	16	14	15	22
Major injuries	120	91	82	46	69	82
Minor injuries	2695	2470	2398	2297	2336	2439
All casualties	2850	2591	2496	2357	2420	2543

by rail.[89] This means that even though the risk/kilometre travelled by rail is higher than for road travel, the fact that people travel less by rail than by road means that their risk exposure is related more to their road travel than to their rail travel. The figures also show that there would have to be a dramatic investment in rail transport if it is to take over a significant part of the travelling done by road. The main exception to this generalisation is people that have to travel into the centre of major conurbations.

As with all forms of transport, train accidents — not all of which result in casualties — have many causes. In 1991–92 there were 960 train accidents. The primary causes of these accidents were: staff error 16%; irresponsible action by the public 41%; technical defects 25%; other causes 11%; miscellaneous undetermined causes 7%.[90] A more detailed breakdown of the causes is given in Table 47.

Air

Air travel takes many forms: UK operators; foreign operators; domestic flights; international flights; scheduled flights; and non-scheduled flights. Taking this whole matrix of forms, in 1994, 109·4 million passengers either arrived at or departed from the United Kingdom.[91] Of these passengers, 47% passed through Heathrow, 19% through Gatwick and 34% through other airports. In all, these passengers flew 171 billion kilometres, 97% of which was on international flights.[92] Table 48 shows something of the incidence of accidents to UK registered aircraft in UK

Table 47. Primary causes of train accidents in Britain during 1991/92[90]

Cause	Collisions	Derailments	Running into obstructions	Fires	Other accidents
Staff error, such as: passing signals, irregularities or want of care by drivers, guards and signalmen, other staff and faulty loading	58	51	31	4	14
Technical defects, such as: trains, track, signal equipment, overhead line equipment, other structures, combined defects, and traction and braking shoes	4	77	11	146	2
Irresponsibility of the public, such as: irregular opening of doors, at level crossings, malicious and other	119	2	159	64	45
Other causes, such as: snow, landslides, floods, animals on line, etc.,	0	3	103	1	0
Miscellaneous and cause not determined	6	11	36	10	3
Total for each type of consequence	187	144	340	225	64
Total no. accidents, all causes			**960**		

airspace in recent years.[93] Table 49 shows the tremendous difference in the number of fatalities in air transport in different parts of the world.[94] Table 50 shows the pattern of accidents involving UK registered aircraft in foreign airspace.[95] Table 51 completes the picture by showing the pattern of accidents involving aircraft registered overseas in UK airspace.[96]

These tables give an indication of real losses, but in aviation there are also statistics about reported near misses. These are cases where the pilot considers his/her aircraft might have been endangered by the proximity of another aircraft. The pilot reports such events on the basis of his/her judgement of the risk involved. Table 52 shows the pattern of near misses reported in recent years.[97]

On a worldwide basis, the number of fatal accidents to scheduled and non-scheduled flights fell from 82 in 1994 to 66 in 1995, and the number

Table 48. Fatalities caused by accidents to UK registered aircraft in UK airspace[92]

Type of aircraft	Fatalities				
	1990	1991	1992	1993	1994
Airline fixed wing aircraft					
crew	0	0	2	2	1
passengers	0	0	0	0	0
third party	1	0	0	1	0
Rotary wing					
crew	2	0	2	0	0
passengers	4	0	11	0	0
third party	0	0	2	0	0
Air taxis					
crew	0	0	0	1	0
passengers	0	0	0	0	0
third party	0	0	0	0	0
Other aircraft (general, commercial)					
crew	17	15	13	11	18
passengers	14	5	8	9	9
third party	1	0	0	0	0
Overall total	39	20	38	24	28

Table 49. Air transport fatalities in different parts of the world[94]

Area	Number of fatalities per 1 000 000 passengers
Africa	14·93
Caribbean/South America	9·93
Former Soviet Union	2·33
Middle East/Asia/Pacific	1·3
Europe	0·74
North America	0·7

of fatalities fell from 1200 in 1994 to 1100 in 1995.[98] There is considerable variation from year to year and there is not always a fall in the number of fatalities. For example, from January to the end of October 1996 there were 32 accidents involving western-built commercial jet airliners, resulting in 883 fatalities.[99]

Following the crash in 1996 of a 27 year old DC9 belonging to a discount fare airline, there was concern that old aircraft were more likely

Table 50. Fatalities caused by accidents to UK registered aircraft in foreign airspace[95]

Type of aircraft	Fatalities				
	1990	1991	1992	1993	1994
Airline fixed wing aircraft					
crew	0	0	0	0	0
passenger	0	0	0	0	0
third party	1	0	0	0	0
Air taxis					
crew	0	0	0	0	0
passenger	0	0	0	0	0
third party	0	0	0	0	0
Other aircraft (general, commercial)					
crew	2	2	1	3	1
passenger	3	0	0	0	0
third party	0	0	0	0	0
Overall total	6	2	1	3	1

Table 51. Fatalities caused by accidents involving aircraft registered overseas in UK airspace[96]

Type of aircraft	Fatalities				
	1990	1991	1992	1993	1994
Airline fixed wing aircraft					
crew	0	0	0	0	5
passenger	0	0	0	0	0
third party	0	0	0	0	0
Other aircraft (general, commercial)					
crew	3	1	1	0	2
passenger	0	0	2	0	2
third party	0	0	0	0	0
Overall total	3	1	3	0	9

to be unsafe than new aircraft. The Federal Aviation Administration is quoted as saying that, 'As long as an aircraft is properly maintained, it is a safe aircraft'.[100] Another view of the safe life of an aircraft was expressed by the head of transport finance of a Japanese bank when he stated that an aircraft has a working life of 25 to 30 years if looked after

Table 52. Pattern of near misses reported in recent years[97]

Type of near miss	Year				
	1990	1991	1992	1993	1994
Total near misses civil and military					
definite risk	25	21	22	12	12
possible risk	51	53	39	66	51
Commercial aircraft					
definite risk	6	0	1	1	2
possible risk	6	5	2	6	13
Commercial air transport aircraft risk bearing near misses per 100 000 hours flown in UK	2	0·7	0·4	0·9	1·6

properly.[100] In addition, he added that his bank did not finance the lease of aircraft which were 15 years old. Following the 1996 crash, the view was expressed in the influential magazine *Time* that perhaps people were willing to accept a higher risk in order to have a lower fare.[101] The view might have been put forward to stimulate discussion of the relationship between acceptable cost and acceptable risk. Certainly, such an argument is an important part of the foundation on which a philosophy of risk has to be built.

Table 53 shows the fleet size and average age of aircraft, and Table 54 shows the size, average age of the jet aircraft fleet, number of departures and accident rate per 100 000 departures, of a selection of airlines in the USA.[100–102] The data in the table show that older aircraft fleets do not always have higher accident rates, so other factors must be involved. Another way of looking at the accident rates is to relate them to whether or not the aircraft type is still in production. It has been

Table 53. Average age of aircraft and size of fleet

Geographical area	Fleet size	Average age in years
North America	5900	15·3
Europe	2953	10·2
Asia	2132	9·9
Central and South America	812	18·4
Africa	510	18·9
Australia	277	10·8

Table 54. *Average age of jet aircraft fleet of a selection of airlines in the USA*[98, 100]

Airline	No. of aircraft (Jan. 1996)	Average age of fleet in years	No. of departures	Accident rate per 100 000 departures 1990–96
American	608	9·20	5 622 932	0·338
Continental	325	13·50	3 150 349	0·349
Delta	480	11·40	6 162 160	0·308
Northwest	380	19·00	3 477 273	0·173
Southwest	226	2·10	3 233 102	0·217
TWA	220	19·70	1 763 784	0·227
United	568	11·50	4 651 020	0·452
US Air	397	12·00	5 782 745	0·242
Valujet	48	25·90	118 264	4·228

suggested that the accident rate is higher for aircraft types that are no longer in production.[103] In the case of the USA, it has been reported that the hull loss rate for aircraft types still in production is one loss per 10·77 million departures, and for aircraft types no longer in production there is one loss per 1·49 million departures. In the case of the rest of the world, the comparable rates are one loss per 0·99 million and one loss per 0·29 million departures. There seems to be a dramatic difference in loss rate between countries themselves and between aircraft types that are in production and no longer in production. It is reported that the accident rate of regional airlines in the USA is much higher than the majors, being about 5 per million departures, and that the Federal Aviation Authority (the US regulatory body) is being pressed to raise the safety standards of small scheduled airlines.[104]

The discussion so far has not exhausted all the risk variables that are associated with air travel. It has been stated that although approach and landing account for only about 4% of flight time, 41% of accidents occur during this phase of the flight.[99] The majority of the accidents on approach were on non-precision approaches, i.e. without the modern landing aids found in major airports. Another feature of the pattern of aircraft accidents is that the so-called Group 2 nations, namely South American, African and a large part of the Asian countries, account for 16% of air traffic but suffer 70% of the losses. In the 12 months from 1 November 1995, insurance claims for losses amounted to 500 million US dollars.

This concern has been given considerable emphasis by the International Federation of Airline Pilots' Association which covers 100 000 pilots in 90 countries. They have warned that the safety of air traffic is critically deficient in the African-Indian Ocean region and claim that 75% of the area's air traffic control systems cannot cope with the present level of traffic.[94]

An element of risk comparison is given by comparing the worldwide 1100 fatalities in aircraft accidents in 1995 with the estimated 500 000 people worldwide (excluding China) who die annually on the road.[100] A better comparison is given by considering a wider range of non-natural causes of death rather than just those resulting from car and aircraft accidents.

Table 55 identifies the number of non-natural causes of death in the United States of America in 1993. The table shows that in 1993 there were 1640 times more deaths due to suicide than due to being an airline passenger. Also the number of car passenger deaths was 1127 times greater than the number of air passengers killed. Fewer bus passengers were killed than airline passengers. The figures are not completely comparable as not everyone has the same degree of exposure, not as many travel by air as travel by road, and there is considerable variation between years in the number of accidents.

Quite apart from the somewhat dry statistics of aircraft accidents, the aircraft industry is, because of its relatively rapid growth, a good example

Table 55. Number of deaths in the USA due to non-natural causes in 1993[102]

Cause of death	No. of deaths
Suicide	*31 102*
Homicide	25 653
Car passenger	21 414
Falls	13 141
Poisoning	7 877
Fire	3 900
Drowning	3 807
Misadventure of surgical, medical care	2 724
Inhalation and ingestion of food	1 186
Struck by falling object	714
Electric current	548
Railway passenger	58
Venomous plants and animals	57
Dog bite	20
Scheduled airline passenger	*19*
Bus passenger	14

of the technical response to risk reduction. Many technical developments led to the reduction of the number of fatalities associated with UK scheduled services falling from 1 per million miles in the mid 1920s to one hundredth of that rate in the 1960s.[105] Quite a lot of this reduction in risk was due to improvements in structural integrity and the improved reliability of engines. Important factors that led to the improved structural integrity were

- better understanding of acceleration loads and their frequency distribution
- better understanding of the properties of materials used
- adoption of multipath fail-safe structures in which cracks could occur without serious reduction of the overall strength.[106]

The whole process of understanding the reliability of aircraft and improving their ability to withstand fault conditions has been underpinned by use of various statistical methods including probability theory and fault analysis. This led to criteria of acceptability being expressed in quantitative terms such as catastrophic failure should not occur more than once in 10^7 landings.[107]

Sea

United Kingdom international passenger sea transport is mainly between Britain and France. In fact such travel accounts for 73·5% of British passenger traffic by sea. Travel between Britain and all European ports accounts for 99% of all British passenger traffic by sea. Table 56 shows the distribution of British passenger traffic over five years from 1990–94.

Passenger ships make up only a small proportion of the fleet of commercial ships. The number of ships registered under United Kingdom or Crown dependency flags has decreased dramatically over recent years. Table 57 compares the composition of the UK registered fleet over the years 1990–94 with the fleet registered in 1986.

Shipping is not without fatalities, but there tend to be considerable variations in the year to year fatality rate. Table 58 shows the number of fatalities in UK registered vessels and the peaks in losses following the loss of the *Herald of Free Enterprise* and the *Marchioness*.

Assessing the significance of transport risks

To understand the significance of risks in transport it is helpful to consider how they are likely to influence policy. The aim of transport policy will

Table 56. UK international sea passenger movements, 1990–1994[108]

Country	1990	1991	1992	1993	1994
Belgium	3588	3510	3239	2958	2878
France	20 104	21 248	22 874	24 643	27 224
Irish Republic	2773	3037	3123	3407	3478
Netherlands	2524	2610	2693	2550	1987
Other EC countries	668	631	575	801	896
Other European countries	431	384	408	354	305
Rest of the world	21	33	26	37	42
Pleasure cruises	153	172	138	193	236
All sea passenger movements	30 263	31 625	33 076	34 943	37 046

Table 57. Ships of 500 gross tons and over registered under UK and Crown dependency flags in 1986 and the years 1990–1994[109]

Number	1986	1990	1991	1992	1993	1994
Tankers	165	123	124	108	106	113
Bulk carriers	73	39	32	30	22	14
Specialised carriers	21	19	18	13	13	13
Cellular container	47	39	32	28	26	34
Ro-Ro	104	93	96	91	86	84
Other general cargo	128	105	99	84	82	93
Passenger	8	9	8	9	9	9
Total	546	427	409	363	344	360
Gross tons (thousands)						
Tankers	3249	2210	2166	2188	2161	2481
Bulk carriers	2003	828	489	446	293	294
Specialised carriers	95	118	99	100	124	110
Cellular container	1369	1275	1091	1015	1017	1236
Ro-Ro	561	555	604	632	657	874
Other general cargo	510	257	242	174	145	212
Passenger	259	269	271	276	272	281
Total	8046	5512	4963	4831	4670	5488

generally be to promote the efficiency of the transport market and its contribution to the economy, to conserve the environment, and to promote transport safety and the mobility of disabled people.

Table 58. Fatalities in UK registered vessels in the period 1984–1994[110]

	1984	1985	1986	1987*	1988	1989†	1990	1991	1992	1993	1994
Deaths from casualties to vessels	3	1	0	190	6	53	6	0	2	0	0
Deaths from accidents on board other than casualties to vessels	11	10	14	8	8	7	0	8	2	3	1
Other deaths including missing at sea, suicides and homicide	5	2	2	5	0	2	0	1	1	0	0
Total	19	13	16	203	14	62	6	9	5	3	1

* Includes the fatalities associated with the loss of the passenger ferry *Herald of Free Enterprise* in which 151 passengers and 38 crew members died.
† Includes the fatalities associated with the loss of the *Marchioness* in the River Thames in which 50 people died.

Generally, such a policy requires an overall integrated transport strategy with clear delineation of responsibilities for development of the various forms of transport, greater individual responsibility in making travel choices and an awareness of the need to make sure that the choices available are those likely to ensure that the economy grows in an environmentally acceptable way.

While there has been general agreement that reductions in pollution and energy use are necessary, there is still no consensus on specific targets. Recent EC directives stipulate the following reductions

- carbon monoxide emissions to be reduced by at least 30% by 1996
- hydrocarbons and NOXs to be reduced by at least 57% in the same time
- SO_2 to be cut to 80% of 1980 levels by 2010
- VOCs to be cut to 30% of 1988 levels by 1999.

Table 59 summarises the guidance the World Health Organisation has given on the levels of pollutants. Reducing pollution is not the only element of transport policy, there is also direct action to reduce the incidence of accidents. Much of transport accident prevention action is aimed at all users, such as licensed users, licensed vehicles, ships and

increase risk. An example of this possibility is shown by the current concern that US Aviation Regulations increase the probability of mid air collisions. To overcome this problem, it has been proposed that the Federal Aviation Regulations should be modified.[115] Modification of regulations takes time, so it could be that there is a period during which people who are following regulations are exposing themselves and others to higher risks than is necessary.

Conclusions

The overall conclusion suggested by this examination of transport risks is that assessment of the acceptability of transport risks has to take into account the user, the vehicle involved and the operating environment. The user has to be competent. The vehicle, no matter whether it is a car, truck, ship or aeroplane, has to be fit for its purpose. The transport operating environment, no matter whether it is road, rail, water or air, has to be organised in a way that keeps risks to an acceptable minimum. The scale of the operations involved means that some form of official regulation is required to keep the associated risks to an acceptable level, but the efficiency of the regulations must be kept under review. Priority for risk control has to be allocated on the basis of the magnitude of the risk, identification of the source of the risk, resources available to take appropriate action and the public pressure for action. It has to be recognised that there is a problem in identifying consistent units for comparing the magnitude of risks associated with various forms of transport. Also, in making comparisons, it has to be remembered that all forms of transport are not really practical alternatives — a bicycle is not an alternative to an aeroplane as a means of crossing the Atlantic.

As the volume of transport used increases, the number of accidents will also increase unless action is taken to reduce their incidence either by improving reliability or by imposing stricter regulation. This raises the question, discussed further in later chapters, of whether it is the number of accidents or the frequency of accidents that is critical in judgements about acceptability?

8

Risks in sport

This chapter examines the statistics relating to risks in sport, and from the results of the examination attempts to draw conclusions about the overall costs and benefits. Attention is concentrated on amateur sport and is drawn to the uncertainties associated with the data used. Finally the implications of sports risks are examined to try and identify what, if anything, they suggest about the acceptability of risks in general.

In this chapter the implications of risks in sports are compared with the risks described in earlier chapters, and an attempt is made to identify how the acceptability of sports risks differs from the acceptability of other types of risk. In our examination of the nature of risk in sport we wanted to avoid anecdotal evidence about major injuries suffered by great sporting stars. Our aim was to concentrate on hard quantitative evidence and for this we have drawn heavily on a Sports Council study.[116] Sports risks are examined under four headings

- the nature of the Sports Council statistics
- the findings of the Sports Council study
- analysis of the Sports Council study
- the implications of sports risks.

Nature of the Sports Council's statistics

The study commissioned by the Sports Council was carried out by the Medical Care Research Unit at the University of Sheffield, and is one of the broadest investigations of sports-related injuries and illness. The study was based on a random sample of the population of England and

Table 60. (below and facing). Categories used in the Sports Council's study

1. Vigorous sports and activities		

a. Sports	*i. 'Ball' games*	
	Soccer	Association football, soccer, five-a-side and seven-a-side football
	Badminton	Badminton
	Cricket	Cricket
	Squash	Squash
	Tennis	Tennis
	Hockey	Hockey
	Basketball	Basketball
	Netball	Netball
	Other ball games	American football, ice hockey, nipsy, rounders, hurling, lacrosse, shinty, baseball, softball, racquet ball, korfball, stool-ball, fives, volleyball
	ii. Other vigorous sports	
	Athletics	Track/field, unspecified
	Gymnastics	Gymnastics, trampolining
	Martial arts	Judo, karate, kung fu, tae kwon do, thai-boxing, tai-chi, unspecified, boxing, wrestling, jujitsu, kick boxing, shoriuji, kempo, kendo, ai kido, self-defence
	Climbing	Abseiling, climbing, climbing walls, mountaineering

b. Activities		
	Running (not track)	Jogging, running, marathon, cross-country running, orienteering
	Horse riding	Cross country horse trials, horse riding, jumping, show jumping, polo, pony riding, dressage/training
	Weight lifting	Multi-gym, weight lifting, weight training
	Swimming and diving	Diving, swimming indoors or outdoors
	Keep fit	Aerobics, eurythmics, keep fit, exercises, callisthenics, popmobility, trimnasium, yoga, circuit training/fitness, rowing machine, exercise bike, treadmill, aqua fit, splashdance, aquaerobics
	Water sports	Boating, canoeing/kayak, power-boating, water-skiing, windsurfing, sailboarding, yachting, hydroplaning, rowing, sailing, canoe polo, rafting, jet skiing, surfing, sculboarding, dragon boat racing

c. Other vigorous sports and recreational or fitness activities		
	Rugby training/coaching, football training, cricket nets training, broomball, caving, pot-holing, cycle racing, cycle training, water polo, fell walking/running, skiing, dry slope skiing	

Table 60 — continued

2. *Other sports and activities*

Golf	Golf
Table tennis	Table tennis
Air sports*	Aerobatics, flying, gliding, gyrocopter, hang gliding, micro light, parachuting, parascending, paragliding/hot air ballooning, skydiving
Motor sports*	Drag racing, karting, moto-cross, motor bike racing, motorbike scrambling, motor car racing, rallying, speedway, stock car/banger racing, motoball, motorcycling, speedway pusher
Hunting, shooting and fishing	Clay pigeon shooting, rough shooting, shooting, fishing, hunting, sea-angling, beagling, stalking
Other sports	Bowling (10 pin), bowls, mini-tennis, Danish longball, croquet, skittles, snooker/billiards, archery
Other activities	Cricket umpire, football referee/linesman, rugby referee, basketball referee/coaching, tennis teaching/coaching, dancing, cycling*, mountain-biking,* scuba diving, octo push, snorkelling, walking, rambling, trekking, hiking, alpine walking, ice-skating, sledging/ tobogganing, donkey-riding, showing ponies, horse management/grooming, assault course, gardening, outward bound, majorettes, DIY, war games, carrom board, roller skating, bell ringing, skate boarding, sports teaching, carriage driving, juggling, frisby throwing, metal detecting, drumming, TA, bottle-digging, tug-of-war, camogie, dark ages society

* Some groups of activities such as air sports and motor sports, and activities such as cycling and mountain-biking are included here only because their reporting may not have been complete.

Wales between the ages of 16 and 45 years. The sample was drawn, with the approval of the appropriate administrative and ethical committees, from the Family Practitioner Committee lists between July 1989 and June 1990. The researchers, with the consent of the family doctors, sent postal questionnaires to 28 857 people. There was a 68% reply rate to the questionnaire which yielded 17 564 usable responses. Of these usable responses, 7829 (45%) had taken part in vigorous exercise or sport in the previous four weeks: 1429 of the vigorous exercisers had been injured in the previous four weeks, and they reported 1803 separate injuries in 1705 incidents. In other words, 18% or about a fifth of the people

Table 61. Summary of the nature of injuries reported for vigorous activities

	Cuts and lacerations	Abrasions	Dislocations	Fractures	Sprains and strains	Contusions	Tenderness, swelling, blisters	Burns	Concussion	Unspecified pain	Other	Illness	Unspecified injury	All	0%
Toes and feet	10	6	4	6	37	35	25	1	0	15	1	0	1	141	7·6
Ankles	4	3	0	1	164	17	1	0	0	16	1	0	1	208	11·5
Legs	16	20	1	4	173	49	1	4	0	39	3	0	4	315	16·4
Knees	13	4	8	0	97	22	0	9	0	81	37	0	1	272	16·1
Neck and trunk	0	1	5	7	90	11	0	0	0	17	3	0	4	138	7·3
Back	2	1	4	0	106	14	0	0	0	89	2	0	3	221	12
Arms	1	6	6	3	157	23	4	4	0	32	2	0	6	240	13·2
Hands and digits	16	6	13	9	31	26	6	0	0	1	0	0	2	110	6·4
Head	4	0	0	0	1	4	0	0	5	0	1	0	0	15	0·8
Face and features neck	2	0	0	1	0	9	0	0	0	1	1	0	0	14	0·8
Mouth and teeth	1	2	0	0	0	0	0	0	0	0	0	0	2	5	0·4
Nose	1	0	0	6	1	6	0	0	0	0	1	0	0	15	0·6
Eyes	2	1	0	0	0	7	0	0	0	0	0	0	1	11	0·6
Ears	2	0	0	0	0	1	1	0	0	0	0	0	0	3	0·2
'Illness'	0	0	0	0	0	0	0	0	0	0	0	88	0	88	5·7
Unspecified	0	0	0	0	2	0	0	0	0	6	0	0	0	8	0·4
All	74	50	41	37	859	224	33	18	5	297	52	88	25	1803	100
0%	4·3	3·3	1·8	45·3	45·3	12·2	2·3	1·1	0·3	17·6	2·9	5·7	1·4		

participating in the study and taking part voluntarily in vigorous exercise had been injured in a month.

The sports activities reported in the answers to the questionnaire were categorised under 27 broad headings. The categories are shown in Table 60. It will be seen from the table that under some headings there is a very wide range of activities, some strenuous and some very modest in the demands they make on physical fitness. For example, under *water sports* are included rowing and power boating, and under *other activities* are included cricket umpiring, gardening and assault courses. It is important to notice that the exposure to risk was not the same in all categories of sport considered and some categories included activities with very different levels of risk.

Seventy five percent of the injuries reported occurred in men and half of the men and women injured were in the age group 16–25 years. Twenty nine percent (8·6 million days off work) of the incidents in all vigorous activities occurred in soccer, no other activity gave rise to more than 10% of the injuries. This showed a very skewed distribution of injuries among the sports. Nearly a third of the injuries reported were associated with one sport out of 27 main groups of sports and sporting activities identified in the study. The question must be asked why are people attracted to participating in a sport with a high risk of being injured? We have to admit that we cannot find a satisfactory answer. Popular fitness activities, such as running, weight training and keep fit, each contributed over two million of the total annual number of incidents, though only a third of these resulted in new injuries.

Fifty eight percent of the injury incidents happened with the involvement of another person or object. Two thirds of the incidents resulted in new injuries, the other third resulted in recurrent injuries. Approximately half of all injuries resulted in non-trivial injuries which were potentially serious. The nature of the injuries reported for vigourous activities is summarised in Table 61.

Findings of the Sports Council study[116]

The analysis of the questionnaire replies showed 1995 reported injuries. The distribution of injuries found is shown in Table 62. Eleven percent of the injuries are classified as either other sports or other activities; this heading appears to include water sports, some of which could be classified as vigorous. Table 63 shows that roughly half the accidents were due to extrinsic causes and half due to intrinsic causes. The precise nature of intrinsic causes is far from clear. Perhaps all that can be said is that a

113

Table 62. Injury incidents by activity reported in Sports Council study

Activity	Sample numbers	Proportion (%) of all incidents	Proportion (%) of all incidents in vigorous activities
Other running	157	7·8	9·1
Soccer	457	24·8	28·9
Badminton	86	4·4	5·1
Cricket	69	3·3	3·8
Rugby	83	4·6	5·4
Squash	80	4·1	4·8
Tennis	45	2·2	2·6
Horse riding	41	1·8	2·1
Weight training	122	6·4	7·5
Keep fit	151	6·4	7·5
Martial arts	85	4·4	5·1
Swimming & diving	83	3·9	4·5
Hockey	39	1·8	2·1
Basketball	16	0·8	0·9
Netball	17	0·7	0·8
Other ball games	28	1·2	1·4
Athletics	9	0·5	0·5
Climbing	10	0·5	0·5
Gymnastics	11	0·5	0·6
Water sports	57	2·9	3·3
Other vigorous activities	59	2·9	3·3
All vigorous activities	*1705*	*85·9*	*100*
Golf	33	1·6	
Air sports	8	0·4	
Motor sports	6	0·2	
Table tennis	4	0·3	
Hunting, shooting & fishing	9	0·4	
Other sports	14	0·7	
Other activities	204	9·9	
Not known	12	0·7	
Total for all activities	*1995*	*100*	

large proportion of the accidents are due to people bumping into each other or bumping into things.

What is the cost of such accidents? In the Sports Council's report, it was estimated that sports accidents resulted in about 11·5 million days' work lost in England and Wales. The cost in lost production

Table 63. Proportion of intrinsic and extrinsic causes of injuries identified in Sports Council report

How occurred	Incidents resulting in new injuries		Incidents resulting in recurrent injuries	
	Sample numbers	Proportion (%)	Sample numbers	Proportion (%)
Extrinsic				
Struck by ball	60	5·3	3	0·5
Struck by other object	37	3·6	0	0
Fall	123	10·8	20	3·4
Collision with furniture	115	10·6	17	2·9
Collision with person(s)	271	26·1	46	8·6
Intrinsic				
Not known	473	43·9	515	84·5
All	*1094*	*100*	*611*	*100*

was estimated to be of the order of £575 million and the cost of treatment £421 million. These calculations do not include any allowance for improved health due to exercise. They represent about one fifteenth of the cost of industrial accidents mentioned in chapter 6. Put another way they represent a cost approximately equal to 0·1% of the countries' GDP.

To put the number of fatal accidents associated with various sports on a comparative basis, Table 64 gives an estimate of fatal accident rates based on the data in ref. 117. For a limited range of sporting activities Table 65 shows the variation in fatal accident rate for three age groups and Table 66 shows the variation in fatal accident rate for men and women.

Our general opinion of the Sports Council's study is that, although it provides a lot of interesting data about the risks in sport, it leaves many important questions still to be answered. These questions include why people choose to participate in particular sports, and can anything be done to reduce the risks? There are trite answers, such as enjoying the challenge and the thrill of winning; such answers are not really satisfactory and the complete answer is probably quite complex involving many factors. It might also be influenced by the fact that vigorous exercise can reduce the risk of a heart attack as compared with a non-exerciser.

Table 64. Fatal accident rates per 100 million occasions (days) of participation for all persons aged 15+ 1982–1989, England and Wales, by activity[117]

Activity	Number of fatal accidents (including drowning)	Estimated death rate (1)	95% confidence interval
Air sports	102	>640 (2)	(>510,–)
Climbing (3)	88	>793	(>440,–)
Motor sports	99	146	(130, 190)
Sailing (4)	33	44·5	(35, 72)
Fishing	104	37·4	(29, 43)
All other water sports (5)	103	67·5	(52, 77)
Rugby (6)	12	15·7	(10, 33)
Soccer	34	3·8	(2·6, 5·3)
Cricket	5	3·1	(1·0, 7·3)
Hockey	1	2·9	(0·1, 17)
Self-defence (7)	3	1·4	(0·3, 4·5)
Boxing/wrestling	3	5·2	(1·0, 14)
Fencing	1	>6·3	(>0·0, –)
Ice-skating	3	4·7	(1·0, 14)
Horse riding (8)	97	34·3	(27, 41)
Track & field athletics	1	1	(0·0, 5·8)
Other running (9)	18	1·2	(0·7, 2·0)
Weightlifting (10)	3	0·2	(0·0, 9·1)
Gymnastics	4	4·8	(1·1, 11)
Squash	4	0·9	(0·3, 2·5)
Tennis	2	0·7	(0·1, 2·8)
Badminton	0	0	(0·0, 0·8)
Table tennis	1	0·2	(0·0, 1·3)
Golf	1	0·1	(0·0, 0·9)
All other activities	77		
Total fatal accidents	799		

(1) Assuming a population of 40 million persons aged 15+. (2) Participation estimated from 1966 data. (3) Including mountaineering and abseiling, but excluding mountain walking, hiking and fellwalking. (4) Including sailing, yachting and dinghy sailing only. (5) E.g. windsurfing, boating, canoeing but excluding swimming and diving. (6) Including union and league but excluding touch rugby. (7) Excluding boxing, fencing and wrestling. (8) Excluding hunting and polo (not included in ref. 117). (9) Including jogging, cross-country, marathon, relay, fun run and roadracing. (10) Including weight training. 'All other activities' excludes 226 deaths during swimming or diving, and 23 deaths during pedal cycling as the numbers are unreliable. Deaths during leisure (rather than sports) activities such as bird-nesting and spectating are also excluded. Deaths during hunting and polo are included in 'all other activities'.

Table 65. *Fatal accident rates per 100 million occasions (days) of participation for different age groups by activity*

Activity	15–24	25–44	45+
Other running	1	1·1	2·2
Soccer	2·5	3·8	26
Rugby	15·4	12·7	<0·1
Cricket	2·5	3·9	<0·1
Fishing	30·4	35	44·6
Sailing	12·6	35	83·3
Horse riding	19·8	33·1	78·7
Squash	<0·1	0·8	3·9
Motor sports	97·5	167·5	687·5
Climbing	787	1263·9	210·5

Table 66. *Fatal accident rates per 100 million occasions (days) of participation for men and women by activity*

Activity	Men	Women
Other running	1·5	<0·1
Fishing	39·3	<0·1
Sailing	45·4	36·9
Horse riding	62·2	29·5
Squash	0·8	1·2
Motor sports	158·5	33·1
Climbing	781·9	663·6

Analysis of the Sports Council study

There are several ways of looking at the risks associated with sport. They are to a large extent voluntary, although those striving for winning may not be able to escape being driven exceptionally hard by over-enthusiastic coaches. Even games such as golf, that for many players makes only modest demands on physical fitness, have some associated risks. It has been suggested rather picturesquely that golfers are more likely than the idle to find themselves in an orthopaedic or cardiac ward.[118] The problems are mainly associated with the intrinsic nature of the golf swing.

The risks associated with contact sports are greater. The risk of real damage is obvious in contact sports such as boxing, wrestling and the martial arts. In some other sports, like motor sport, there is a risk that the equipment may fail or behave in an abnormal way which results in the participants being hurt or killed. In general, sports involving dependence on the reliability and proper use of equipment such as cars,

117

aeroplanes and climbing gear have risks many times greater than those associated with sports such as golf or tennis.

The Sports Council's study really only examined the incidence of injuries due to sports. It does not attempt a risk assessment of the type that would be expected to justify the acceptability of any industrial activity. Any detailed risk assessment of a sport would have to examine all the components of the sport and determine if they met some agreed risk acceptability criteria or if action was required to reduce the risk. The components of a sport that should be considered in a risk assessment may, depending on the sport, include

- criteria for acceptability
- possible causes of injury and their incidence
- action that can be taken to reduce the level of the inherent risks
- how can the action required to make the risk level acceptable be initiated and implemented.

Identifying the causes of injury would go well beyond the simple list given in Table 62 and would include

- adequacy of protection used
- potential of contact with ground or other substances contaminated with toxic materials[119]
- failure of equipment
- collision, either accidental or intentional, with any other participant
- adverse weather conditions
- unsuitable venue
- adequacy of skill and fitness of participants
- adequacy of management and general organisation of the event.

The above list shows that assessment of risks associated with any sport would have many characteristics common to any risk assessment.

Implications of sports risks

Sports risks have a rather different character to the more corporate risks considered in the earlier chapters. Acceptance of sports risks is very much a matter of individual choice. Although there is an element of corporate risk in the organisation of sporting events. Major events often represent very large investments, for example, the risk of the Olympic Games in Atlanta in 1996 having to be abandoned was insured for US$200 million and the Wimbledon tennis tournament was insured for £57 million.[120] Another aspect of sports injuries is that they lead to the loss of 11 million working days a year.[121] Companies often provide sporting facilities for their employees, partly to develop team spirit and *esprit de corps*. This does give rise to some interesting legal questions that do not seem to be fully resolved.[121] The questions include whether employees can claim damages from their employer if they are hurt in a match in which they are representing the company and playing on a company owned facility.

In general, individuals make up their own minds about the acceptability of participating in a particular sport. In schools and some other organisations there may be an element of coercion to participate in sport and there may even be coercion about which sport in which to participate. Having selected the sport in which to participate, the individual is surrounded by rules and conventions about the way the sport will be played. Some of the rules are designed to reduce the risks to which participants are exposed. Some rules are devised by international bodies, some by national bodies and some on almost an *ad hoc* basis by clubs. At major professional events it is likely that there will be very careful adherence to the rules. At club level there is likely to be a more relaxed approach to precisely implementing rules, perhaps because there is a shortage of people with a detailed knowledge of the rules, and perhaps because there are people who are new to the sport and are not aware of the rules.

Also sometimes, as in any group, there will be mavericks who will intentionally flout rules for their own advantage or simply to satisfy their own ego.

In many ways participation in sport is based upon the individual's perception of the acceptability of the risks and benefits involved and trust in the people organising the sport. There is not a lot of information on the extent to which people participating in hazardous sports take notice of warnings about the magnitude of the risk to which they are exposed. In the general sense it is appreciated that hazard perception is a key affecting behaviour.[122] However, there is one interesting study of the response of rock climbers to hazard warnings.[123] The study examined the response of 892 climbers to warnings of risk — the results of the study showed that climbers of greater ability responded less to warnings than climbers of lower ability. The results also showed that the greater the hazard the greater the response. Although climbers with the greatest technical ability tend to tackle the most physically demanding climbs they do tend to heed advice and take the easiest way of tackling a difficult climb. This suggests that even though climbing has the highest death rate associated with it (Table 64), some people are willing to take the risks and even to ignore warnings.

In some sports such as motor racing, flying, climbing and equestrian sports, participation involves large costs, and participation is therfore limited by economic factors. The economic risks are also indicated in another way: people participating in high risk sports find it difficult to obtain insurance cover and if they can obtain cover they have to pay a heavily weighted premium.

On the positive side, there have been improvements in medical techniques that help nature to repair damaged ligaments, tendons and muscles and generally to speed recovery.[124]

Overall, sports risks could be characterised as the one type of risk where people train to minimise the impact of the risk.

9

Assessment of risk acceptability

In this chapter, an approach to the assessment of risks inherent in a wide range of activities is developed. Starting from a simple model, an optimum method of assessing risk acceptability is built up which, it is postulated, is an appropriate tool for comprehensive assessment of risks. The proposed method pays particular attention to dealing with the uncertainties that are inevitably a part of such decision-making.

Introduction

Two topics that have not been explored so far are

- the decision-maker's concept of the degree of risk that is acceptable to achieve a particular end
- how the acceptability of a risk can be assessed.

We all know of people who will bet on horses that are at long odds and have little chance of winning, and of people who will invest money from a very limited family budget in a lottery ticket with a very small chance of winning a prize. It is also true that in the world in general, decision-makers do not all have the same opinion about the degree of risk they will accept. Some decision-makers, such as those associated with insurance or banking might relate their flexibility in accepting a risk to the price they charge for accepting it, but while there may be a degree of flexibility, there is generally a clear limit to the risk they will accept. For example, an insurer may not be willing to provide life cover, even at a high premium, for someone beyond a certain age or suffering

Table 67. The variables associated with forms of committee decision-making

Form of committee	Significance
Formal board expected just to endorse the recommendations of an executive	This type of board really does not contribute anything to the quality of the decision, but if things go wrong may be held responsible. For such a board to be a success it must embody all the skills required to assess the full range of factors involved
An investigative board expected to perform its own assessment of the acceptability of the options	Provided the board has the appropriate skills to really assess in depth all the technical, economic and socio-political factors involved, such a board can be very effective. To be fully effective such a board would need responsibility and capability to monitor the progress of a project and initiate any corrective action found to be necessary
A financial control board with responsibility to approve and provide funding for proposals, but not the skills or support to effectively assess the acceptability of proposals	This is just a financial control board and does not have the necessary multidisciplinary skills to make a comprehensive assessment of all the factors that influence the acceptability of a proposal. The decisions by such a board may prove to be disastrous
A board with responsibility to approve, fund and control proposals and with all the required skills and powers	This is the most effective type of board, but in practice some of its control responsibilities may have to be delegated to others. The overall success of the board depends on the quality of the people to whom such control responsibilities are delegated

considered in chapters 3 to 8 but such a view would be misleading. Table 68 sets out what we regard as the common features and important differences of decision-making in the six sectors considered.

To a greater or lesser extent there is usually a money factor involved — for example, concern about whether or not a particular venture can make a profit — but money is not always the primary component of the decision-making process, and in many sectors the nature of public opinion and the manner in which this is expressed is an important variable that must be considered. For example, a major transport project may be subject to public opinion expressed forcibly by pressure groups demonstrating on site, while in the medical and sports sectors it is the

Table 68. Similarities and differences in decision-making in the six sectors

Sector	Similarities	Differences
Manufacturing sector	Cost, availability of funds, changes in demand. Return on investment.	Wrong decision may lead to firm being closed. Risks due to plant and equipment failure
Financial sector	Cost of lending, return of security for loan, availability of funds. Public support or demand for the particular activity involved.	Ultimately benefits measured just in money terms
Major projects	Availability of funds and appropriate security. Adequacy of return. Public support.	Benefits take many forms which to some extent could be reduced to financial terms. Expression of benefits in money terms may be misleading
Medical	Cost, availability of funds. Likelihood of success. Will the expenditure produce a benefit? Demand from the relevant public.	Although there is a cost factor involved, the primary concern should be whether or not a decision can lead to the patients' condition being improved
Transport	Cost, availability of funds. Benefit from expenditure. Demand from the relevant public.	The amount of improvement possible is related to the funds available. (This includes public willingness to pay taxes or special levies for the work.) Public demand for improvement in transport
Sport	Cost of participation. Particular form of success achieved. Personal decision to participate.	Participation in sport is generally voluntary. Benefit measured by the individual's satisfaction. To a large extent funded by participants. (The increasing role of sponsorship in amateur sport is recognised)

opinions of individuals that are of primary importance. In some cases, individuals' opinions may be overlaid by some form of greater public involvement — such as a political requirement that only certain treatments may be paid for by public funds, or a governing body's specification as to how a sport may be undertaken to keep accidents to a minimum — that will also prescribe the nature of the ultimate decision.

Despite talk about involvement of the democratic process in decision-making, the views of the public are, in reality, rarely sought with precision. Election manifestos of political parties outline only the programmes to be followed, and while countries such as Switzerland quite often employ a referendum procedure to approve specific proposals, this is rarely the case in Britain. Even so, politicians often make decisions based on their own view of what is acceptable, taking into account only those factors which support this view and — especially where a referendum is involved — oversimplifying the options to produce a 'yes/no' answer; in most cases, the public have not had explained to them the full range of options and their implications. The following examples — one from the transport sector and one from the medical field — illustrate the process of 'yes/no' decision-making.

A government may recognise that the road infrastructure is in need of major improvement but, being short of funds, mounts a propaganda offensive designed to shift public opinion from favouring road transport to support for transport by rail. This campaign will overlook or obscure the fact that in order for railways to provide individuals with the same convenience and speed of travel as roads, much greater expenditure would be required and the time taken to raise the standard of the railways to match the current levels of convenience provided by the roads would span several decades. Overlooking or obscuring the factor that is efficient use of travellers' time, amounts to the imposition of an increase in costs stemming from an overall reduction in the efficiency of the economy.

In the medical field one can take the example of a country which has a state health service that deals with all the medical needs of its citizens. In time, the prevailing political philosophy may have altered and, instead of championing an *at cost* service funded through taxation, it believes that a viable service must generate an element of profit to be paid to profit-based, unelected providers and insurance companies. The effect of this shift in philosophy is to require people to bear responsibility for their medical needs and buy insurance to cover them.

Both of these examples describe cases which would have a direct impact on people's lives and where public opinion should, therefore, have an important influence on the decisions. Ignoring public opinion in these cases could lead to decisions of doubtful value and certainly to decisions of doubtful acceptability to the public.

A word of caution: public opinion is not always right! Moreover, it has to be recognised that public opinion is a variable factor, which in one area or at one time may be in favour of accepting a particular level of risk, but in another area or at another time may demand that risk should be kept at a lower level.[126] In public discussion of acceptability it is not unknown for significantly differing views about the acceptability of the risks involved to be presented; some groups may amplify the magnitude of the risk while others may reduce its importance. An interesting example of the way amplification of the risk can occur was identified in a study of the decision on where to locate high level radioactive waste.[127] The media tended to exaggerate the risks associated with nuclear generating plant while the public focused on economic impact and claimed that property values and business activity would fall. In practice, demand for housing and housing valuations had been rising in localities of some nuclear generating plant and business activity had been increasing.

All of this serves to underline how important it is for those concerned with or involved in decision-making to appreciate the implications of all the decision options; the complex reasons for differences in perception of risk are not properly understood and the author of ref. 127 is not alone in calling for more research in this area.

Our own views on the highest acceptable level of risk in a wide variety of situations is in the range of probability that the unacceptable risk will occur from 10^{-3} to 10^{-4} times per year, although we accept that uncertainty about the quality of the data that must be used may require the level of risk to be set lower. When making an assessment of the acceptability of the risks associated with a particular project, the decision-maker must allow for uncertainty both in the data and in the views about what is an acceptable risk. The assumption that the uncertainty is evenly distributed about some mean value can be misleading, because in many cases the data themselves may have a skewed distribution about the mean. Nevertheless, the decision may have to be made without the decision-maker having any precise information about the form of distribution of the available data.[128]

This chapter is built on the basic assumption that the decision-maker will be concerned to determine which of the options under consideration is associated with the most acceptable level of risk and whether that risk can be reduced still further; he/she will be interested in the whole spectrum of risks — technical, economic and socio-political — that could in some way influence a successful outcome. The following methodology for assessing the acceptability of risk involves four stages

(a) describing a simple model of the decision-making process
(b) identifying the significance of the factors involved and the uncertainties associated with their evaluation
(c) suggesting alternative ways of assessing multivariate problems
(d) postulating the optimum method of assessing risk acceptability.

A simple model of the risk decision process

A simple generalised model, whose form is influenced by the array of statistics identified in earlier chapters, is postulated as the starting point for developing a universally applicable methodology for the assessment of risk acceptability. The aim is a comprehensive assessment of all the factors that influence risk acceptability; the method of analysis adopted has its origins in earlier work of Chicken[129, 130] and recognises Arrow's work on preference and choice.[131]

We begin by postulating a simple model of the decision-making process which, as the chapter develops, is progressively refined so that by the end of the chapter it represents a practical aid that can be tailored to the determination of the acceptability of the risks inherent in most types of proposal. It is not intended to restrict the type of proposal considered to any particular type of activity; the approach is designed to be flexible so that it can be adapted for application to a wide spectrum of activities. A diagrammatic representation of the simple model appears in Fig. 10.

The decision-making process is described in the model as an engine which converts various inputs into a decision. It is appreciated that, in reality, the decision-making process involves many subtle interactions, but at this stage in the discussion it is convenient simply to consider

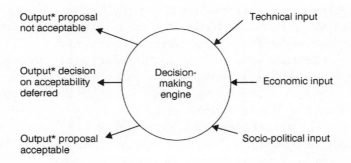

* The decision-making engine will produce only one output for each proposal

Fig. 10. A simple model of the risk acceptability decision-making process

that three inputs provide the fuel that enables the engine to produce a decision.

The decision-making process is particularly well suited to being described as an engine because both are complex organisms which perform the function of converting a raw input into a more useful output. The decision-making engine assesses the input data against criteria it has been programmed to test data against, and makes due allowance for the uncertainties involved. (The identification of clusters of data may be regarded as the preliminary stage in a multivariate analysis;[132] and the problem of integrating assessment of factors that have been measured in different units is addressed later in the chapter.) In other words, the engine processes the available information and determines which decision is justified.

It is important to recognise that an intrinsic feature of all inputs is the uncertainty associated with them and that they cannot be represented by a single unique value. The uncertainty is greatest when a proposal is first launched and generally gets gradually less as the proposal develops, and data is refined, but the uncertainty rarely disappears entirely. It is not intended to suggest that there is some neat linear relationship between the status of a proposal and the associated uncertainty. Uncertainty does not always decrease as a project develops. Dramatic variation in uncertainty may develop in a project particularly when it is a novel project. However, it remains true that as a proposal/project develops the decision-making engine will draw in more data that will tend to improve the understanding of the acceptability of the options available. An important caveat to this view is that the increase in data available to the decision-making engine may show a proposal to be more acceptable or less acceptable. The change that more data makes to acceptability cannot be prejudged. (We do not in any way deny the help that Bayesian methods and statistical inference can be to the decision-maker.)

To illustrate the problem of uncertainty about data, Fig. 11 shows a typical spread of data about the three proposal defining factors of technical, economic and socio-political. Because the three factors are measured in different units their significance is compared on a simple ordinal rating basis. The figure shows how the input data about each factor may be clustered around a particular value. Also, the characteristic of each cluster is different.

The output from the decision-making engine may take any one of the following three forms

(*a*)   reject proposal

129

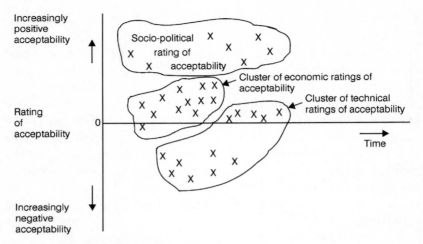

Fig. 11. Clustering of input data

(b) defer decision

(c) accept proposal.

It is accepted that an identical scale of preferences for risk accept-ability will not be used in all decision-making; however, as the methodology described can be adapted to suit any scale of preferences, the generality of the argument is considered to be sound.

Significance of the factors

The assumption is made that each of the factors that must be considered in order to reach a decision falls under one of the following headings

- technical
- economic
- socio-political.

It is possible to argue for the consideration of greater or fewer groupings of factors but we take the view that these three primary groupings adequately describe the range of parameters involved in decision-making; evaluation of each of the primary factors requires the acceptability of all the associated sub-factors to be integrated and in practice, for a major project, there may be several hundred such sub-factors.

Before examining the way in which the significance of the three groups of primary factors can be integrated to give an overall assessment, it is necessary to consider each of them individually.

Technical

There are three important aspects of all technical factors and sub-factors that should be considered

(a)   general risk implications
(b)   risks inherent in the activity
(c)   changes in risk occurring throughout the life of the activity.

Tables 69, 70 and 71 summarise the range of sub-factors that should be included under the heading *technical factors*. The issues identified in the tables additionally start to expose technical issues that may have significant economic implications — particularly if they are the source of the uncertainties associated with the through life value of the project. The nature of the risk implications of economic factors and sub-factors is examined in more detail below.

Economic

Under this heading the following three types of factor are identified

(a)   borrowing
(b)   lending
(c)   increasing value.

Borrowing and lending are single purpose arrangements; they are, therefore, relatively straightforward and their implications are usually

Table 69. General risk implications

Issue	Nature of assessment required
Chance of members of the public being fatally harmed by some form of catastrophic failure of the project	All chains of events that can lead to members of the public being harmed in some way
Failure of the project that leads to members of the public being harmed in some non-fatal way	Determine the magnitude and frequency of such failures
Non-reversible harm to the environment	Establish the nature and magnitude of the harm and the possibility of the harm being prevented

131

Table 70. Risks inherent in the activity

Issue	Nature of assessment required
Will it be possible to bring the project to fruition for the predicted cost?	Will funding be available if project costs more than expected?
Will the project perform as planned?	Quantify the consequences of below specification performance?
Will the project be completed on time?	Quantify the consequences of delays in completing the project?

Table 71. Through life changes in risks

Issue	Nature of assessment required
Will the project last the predicted life?	What is the probability of full life being achieved? What are the consequences of full life not being achieved?
What additional work will be required on the project throughout its life?	What is the probability and likely cost of the additional work that may be required?
What is the chance that the specification the project has to satisfy will change during its predicted life?	What changes may be made to the specification the project has to satisfy and what is the probability that they may be made?

quite clear. Borrowing and lending may both show a financial profit to the borrower and/or the lender.

Increasing value deserves somewhat more explanation because it involves several features of importance to the decision-making process. At the time the contract is drawn up, the profit margin that the lenders hope for is generally clear. However, the final outcome may be different; the borrower may default on the loan or the lender may go bankrupt, causing a loan to be called in early. The borrower's profit is less certain and may not be known until the project or activity for which the funding has been borrowed is complete. Where a simple value increasing activity — such as manufacturing — is involved the total profit will be realised only at the end of the predicted life of the project. Where more complex activities are involved — particularly if these are of a social nature — it may be extremely difficult to calculate the return on the investment. In such cases, an attempt has to be made to estimate the return on

Table 72. Borrowing risks

Issue	Nature of assessment reqiored
Interest rates vary	Can an increase in interest to be paid be accepted?
Lender calling in loan prematurely	Will it be possible to negotiate a loan to replace the one called in without financially embarrassing the project?
Foreign exchange problems on foreign loans	How stable are the currencies and if they increase the cost of the loan can this be afforded?
Inability to pay interest and repayments	Is income required to pay interest and repayments reliable?
Amount borrowed inadequate	How well is financing required known and can additional funds be borrowed?

investment in terms of the through life net benefit — a positive net benefit representing an acceptable return. Many variables have to be allowed for in such evaluations and there is a considerable degree of uncertainty associated with the results from such calculations.

Tables 72 (borrowing), 73 (lending) and 74 (increasing value) summarise the considerations that have to be taken into account in assessing the risks associated with economic factors.

Table 73. Lending risks

Issue	Nature of assessment required
Borrower has income or assets that should allow him/her to pay interest and repay loan	Confirmation required about income and realizable assets of borrower
Borrower has a good credit record	Assessment of credit record and rating of borrower
No better opportunities for lending money at that rate	Market assessment
Borrower lives in a socially, politically and economically stable country	Check stability of country where he/she lives or does business

Table 74. Increasing value risks

Issue	Nature of assessment required
Is process proved?	How well has the system been tested and how did it perform?
Is market for product available?	If a market is available will it be possible to take a share of it? What competition is there?
How long will the market last?	Is there any information about the likely life of the market?
How volatile is the market?	Are the returns when the market is high greater than the returns when the market is low?
What appears to be the trend in market development?	Is the market expanding or contracting?
How long will the life of this process be?	Is some more efficent manufacturing process likely to appear soon?

Socio-political

It is intended that the heading socio-political factors should include all the influences external to a proposal that may affect its public accept-ability. Table 75 summarises our views of the issues likely to be involved and the form of assessment required to determine their significance.

Many of the processes involved in determining the acceptability of risk require elements of trust and credibility between the associated parties. It has been shown that various types of group hold clearly detectable differences of view as to what are the most important influences in establishing trust and credibility.[133] Some of the findings are summarised below.

- For industry
  - care and concern gives the largest increase in perceptions of trust and credibility; information received and disclosed come close second and third factors

- For government
  - commitment and knowledge/expertise are the first and second most important factors in increasing perceptions of trust and credibility

Table 75. Socio-political factor risks

Issue	Nature of assessment required
Public acceptability of proposal	Survey of opinion or voting on issue involved, this should take account of both the views of the people directly involved and the community at large
Public demand	Identifying how strong demand is and what options are there in the way the demand may be satisfied
Proposition not compatible with the programme of the political party in power	Assess whether proposition can be made acceptable to the party in power
If funds are not available for the proposal	Determine if any other source of funding can be found, for example, is a Private Finance Initiative an alternative to government finance

- For citizen groups
  - knowledge/expertise is by far the most important factor in increasing perceptions of trust and credibility and is considered very much more important than commitment.

Alternative ways of assessing multivariate problems

Multivariate problems arise in many fields of endeavour and many ways of solving them have been developed. Elementary solutions consider the variables in pairs and, by an iterative process, determine which are the two or three dominant variables. More thorough, but more complex, are solutions based on computers that attempt to create models to simulate the real world. The fascinating range of computer simulations includes those of national economics as well as simulators for training pilots. The very fact that flight simulators allow pilots to explore situations that would be unsafe in real flight demonstrates the enormous capability of computer simulators to extend the assessment of multivariate problems.

It is not intended to give the impression that all situations can be simulated with absolute precision. Precise simulation depends on an exact knowledge of the relationship between the variables; in reality, particularly in a novel situation, the relationship between the variables may not be known and it is even possible that all the variables involved are not even identified. Examples of such situations are medical drugs and pesticides which have been in use for several years before unacceptable characteristics become manifest. Uncertainty about the variables involved and the relationship between them exposes the magnitude of the uncertainty that must be allowed for in assessing the risks associated with any multivariate situation, although in some cases the methods of fuzzy data analysis may help overcome deficiencies in the precise value of variables and their interaction with one another.

Earlier in this chapter the three main groups of variables associated with assessing risk acceptability were identified as technical, economic and socio-political. It must be emphasised that these three factors are not single variables but that each represents a matrix of associated sub-factors. It therefore follows that assessment of each of the three main groups of factors also requires the assessment of a matrix of sub-factors. In a large project there may be several hundred sub-factors and the first question to ask is whether there is some connection between them that can indicate how their relative importance and significance can be judged.

In very simple terms

$$A = K_1T + K_2E + K_3SP \tag{9.1}$$

where A is a measure of overall acceptability
          T is a measure of technical acceptability
          E is a measure of economic acceptability
          SP is a measure of socio-political acceptability
          and K_1, K_2 and K_3 are constants weighting the
          importance of factors T, E and SP

It may be that the decision-maker considers the risk factors of equal value and K_1, K_2 and K_3 each equal 1; for other proposals other values may be equally justifiable to the decision-maker. However, it is important to remember that if all decisions are to be made in a consistent manner, any system of weighting must be justifiable and applied in a way that is both consistent and defensible. It is also a requirement that justification of the decision process is transparent.

It must also be recognised that the importance of the various factors may be different at different times in the life of a project. It is relatively easy to envisage a stage when perhaps the technical and economic risks are acceptable but that the acceptability of the project in socio-political terms has not been resolved; such a situation is most likely to occur when the overall assessment of individual sub-factors is incomplete. It is also possible to envisage a scenario in which the technical and socio-political aspects of a proposal are acceptable but there is uncertainty about the acceptability of the economic factors; a situation such as this could easily arise if a project were to run out of cash because of some unforeseen technical problem.

The assumption, in equation (9.1), that the importance of the individual factors is additive must also be questioned. It is perhaps difficult to justify the relationship being anything other than additive but it may be possible to construct some ranking or rating of acceptability based on multiplication of the factors. Such a methodology simply requires specification of the relationship between the rating numbers and could give rise to an equation of the form

$$A_c = K_1 T \times K_2 E \times K_3 SP \qquad (9.2)$$

where A_c is a measure of overall acceptability but measured on a different scale to A in equation (9.1)

T, E, SP, K_1, K_2 and K_3 would have the same or similar meaning to that in equation (9.1)

Optimum method of comparing risk acceptability

It should by now be evident that the optimum way of comparing the acceptability of the risks inherent in a group of proposals must, as outlined above, consider all the technical, economic and socio-political factors involved. The list of factors will not be the same for every case but it must contain a sufficient number of factors to demonstrate the fundamental nature of the proposals that are to be considered.

It is generally the case that the factors that must be considered will have been measured in a variety of disparate units; therefore, in order to compare them impartially, it will be necessary to introduce some form of non-dimensional, ordinal ranking. Ordinal ranking allows the significance of disparate factors to be weighted and integrated in consistent terms; in the context of risk assessment, the application of ordinal ranking will provide an overall view of acceptability. Of course, there is always the possibility that ordinal ranking will be abused to distort the assessment of acceptability or that there will be disagreement between the decision makers about how the rating of risk acceptability should be measured. These problems are considered further in the next chapter.

Direct comparison of risks associated with various proposals or options will only be valid if the comparison is made using data of a consistent quality and if the assessments are based on uniform criteria for judging acceptability.

If assessment of risk acceptability is developed as outlined above, we contend that it should provide a valid answer to the questions that are asked about the philosophical soundness of the methodology employed.

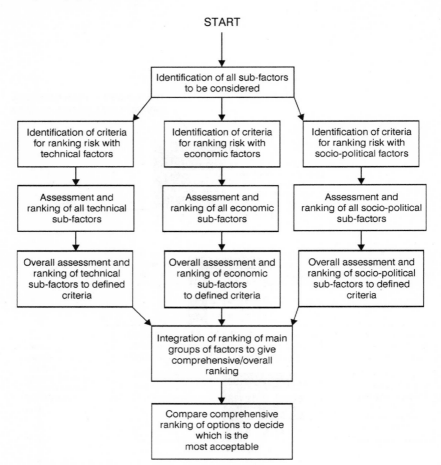

Fig. 14. Summary of the whole comprehensive risk assessment process

There are three critical questions that can be asked about any risk assessment methodology

(a)   What is the logic that enables the assessment of masses of disparate data to be justifiably encapsulated in a simple statement of the acceptability of a risk?

(b)   How is it possible to establish universal criteria for determining the acceptability of risk that fit all situations?

(c)   Is it necessary to make allowance for the decision-maker's perception of risk acceptability when attempting to determine an overall measure of risk acceptability?

Comprehensive risk ranking is one way of assessing acceptability. Figure 12 represents a flow chart for the comprehensive assessment process and Table 76 shows the criteria that could be used to assess the acceptability of the various factors involved. In Table 77 a possible ranking/scoring scale is described, and Fig. 13 shows how the matrix of ranking scores varies with the ranking scores of the individual groups of factors as well as demonstrating the combinations of individual factor scores that identify unacceptable proposals. Attention is drawn to the fact that the scoring scale has been designed so that the significance of one factor having an unacceptable score cannot be masked by other factors having acceptable scores. This feature gives confidence in the impartiality and integrity of the methodology.

The description of the comprehensive risk ranking methodology that has just been given concentrates on the final phase of the assessment of a proposition — the phase when assessment of all the sub-factors involved has been made. To depict, unequivocally, the magnitude of the assessment process, Fig. 14 summarises the whole.

There are certain key steps in the assessment process that are relevant to any risk assessment. These are

Table 76. Nature of the criteria for assessing a ranking factor

Main group factor	Examples of criteria for assessing main group factor	Possible sub-factors that may have to be included in main group factor
Technical	Extent to which proposal will produce required results?	Performance and expected life. Reliability (past experience). Harm to the public
Economic	Extent to which proposal will produce required financial benefit from lifetime expenditure involved. (It is essential that economic acceptability is judged in through life terms as just judging on first cost can give misleading results.)	Supply and demand (for product of proposed activity). Magnitude of possible financial loss. Payoff. Index of harm/benefit. Through life net benefit.
Socio-political	Extent to which proposal is acceptable to the public	Public demand. Results of public Inquiries. Political climate. Views on current quality of life.

Table 77. Ranking scale for acceptability

Rank	Acceptability	Individual group factor score (score of technical, economic and socio-political factors)	Total score range (sum of main group scores)
1	Acceptable without reservation	1	3
2	Requires certain action to make acceptable	2	4–6
3	Considerable action required to make acceptable	5	7–15
4	Not acceptable	14	16–42

- identification of all the sub-factors involved
- collection of all the data required for assessment of the sub-factors
- assessment of the sub-factors
- integrated assessment of the sub-factors to provide an assessment of the three main groups of factors — technical, economic and socio-political
- integrated assessment of the technical, economic and socio-political factors to give an overall, or comprehensive, assessment of the risks associated with the proposition.

It is appreciated that when an assessment starts it may have to be based on qualitative data. This would mean that the uncertainty about the accuracy of the assessment would be considerable and the only solution to this problem is to replace soft, qualitative data by hard, relevant, quantitative data.

10

An overall risk philosophy

This chapter aims to distil the arguments presented in the earlier chapters and to extract a universal philosophy of risk acceptability. At the very least, we see the proposed philosophy to be a way of clarifying thinking about risk acceptability and to provide a useful tool to aid evaluation of risk acceptability. Judgement about the validity of the philosophy is left to the reader.

There are many forms of risk that have not been considered in detail in this study. Vandalism, theft and arson in schools, which in 1992 cost Britain £49 million,[134] have not been addressed and neither have the risks of being subject to violent attack, computer failure, dramatic change in the climate, genetic disaster or becoming deaf or blind. There is also a vast range of unidentified or unforeseen risks — faults in aeroplanes that are found to occur only after hundreds of the particular type of aircraft have been flying for 20 years, or side effects associated with drugs that only manifest themselves after a ten-year period in use — that have come to be accepted as a part of life. Nevertheless, we are confident that the range of risks that has been considered gives a good general indication of the pattern of characteristics of the whole spectrum of risks that exists and shows, in practical terms, that people in different situations accept different levels of risk. Thus, while the human race is faced with a very wide range of risk situations, views as to the acceptability of which are almost equally as varied, a multi-attribute and multidimensional risk philosophy can, we believe, be postulated.

In order to put the arguments that follow into perspective, Lord Ashby's view of decision-making and risk acceptability is a helpful starting point.[135] Ashby's contention was that the process is akin to a chain reaction triggered by the decision-maker's hunch as to what constitutes the best decision. This will be conditioned by the decision-maker's experience relevant to the issue, beliefs about the issue and his/her attitude to those beliefs. Ashby cites the work of Otway and Edwards to substantiate the view that because decision-makers can only take into account between five and nine beliefs at one time they tend to have in mind a simplified model of the issue.[136] This means that the ultimate decision will be the best decision only if the model contains all the beliefs that are critical to the decision, and the decision-maker adheres strictly to the logic of rational decision-making.

For decisions in the public area the weight politicians attach, or fail to attach, to the available evidence, whether hard or soft, is an important factor that has to be taken into account. The political rhetoric used to introduce or defend some new decision or policy often presents untested or untestable hypotheses as if they were objectively predictive.[137] This frequently leads to a proliferation of peer-review panels charged with finding justification for things which cannot be justified, and results in the promotion of some very doubtful views, such as

- the risk of breast cancer can be reduced by modification of dietary fat intake
- trichlorethylene alone is a cancer risk
- fluoridation of drinking water is a risk free way of preventing tooth decay
- the acceptability of the risks inherent in a proposal need be based only on assessment of the economic factors.[137]

All decision-making is also influenced by the decision-maker's propensity for risk or regret avoidance. It is our contention, however, that the propensity towards risk or regret avoidance may be seen as just a part of the process of setting the upper and lower limits of risk acceptability. In our attempt to develop an overall risk philosophy we concentrate primarily on situations where the acceptance or refusal of a risk is based on objective evidence of the significance of all the factors involved. While we do consider cases when the decision has to be based on logically defensible subjective evidence, we hold to the view that decisions based solely on subjective evidence can only be preliminary decisions and that an attempt must always be made to obtain objective evidence before the decision is finalized. This view also implies that the proposer makes no attempt to camouflage subjective evidence so that it will appear to be objective — a practice we consider to be immoral and unjustifiable.

Returning to the concept of decision-making as a chain reaction, it must be recognised that arriving at a decision on a major project may take many years; evidence must be gathered and progressively hardened into a form that provides a sound basis for a decision. Generally, as the process advances, some risks are eliminated and additional risks are exposed, each phase constituting an immutable step towards a particular decision and implying acceptance of a certain level of risk. It is as though the process has a predictable pattern like the growth of a plant.

The rationale presented here endeavours to answer four questions.

(*a*) What is expected from a risk philosophy?
(*b*) Can a universally applicable risk philosophy reveal a level of risk acceptability applicable to all types of risk?
(*c*) Is it possible to develop a universally applicable risk philosophy from the mass of data of the types presented in chapters 3–8, given also that all the variables are not associated with every risk situation and that many of the variables are measured in different units?
(*d*) Is acceptability of risk really determined in a structured way that takes account of the long term benefit or do people simply accept the option that is likely to give the most immediate satisfaction?

Overall view of risk acceptability evidence

The nature of involvement with risk can be considered to comprise any one of the following basic characteristics or some combination of them

- voluntary
- unavoidable
- single consequence
- multi-consequence
- recoverable outcomes
- non-recoverable outcomes.

In Table 78 the six basic characteristics are summarised. Each risk situation will have its own unique characteristics, for example, a risk could be voluntary, multi-consequence and have recoverable outcomes. Table 79 shows how several types of activity can be characterised.

As well as considering variations in the type of risk, there is a hierarchy in risk size that must be considered. The spectrum of risk sizes ranges from very small routine decisions that can be decided in seconds by individuals to very large decisions, involving many people

Table 78. The characteristics of the six main types of risk

Risk	Characteristic
Voluntary	A risk you are not under any form of compulsion to take, e.g. sport, investment, gambling
Unavoidable	A risk you must take as part of your work, e.g. a soldier or a miner do not have any option but to take risks. This heading also includes natural disasters and terrorism
Single consequence	A single consequence risk is very rare, most risks have several direct and indirect consequences
Multi-consequence	Most risks are multi-consequence, some consequences being direct and some indirect. A company failing is an example of a multi-consequence risk. When a company fails several people lose money and are made poorer and jobs are lost
Recoverable outcomes	Recoverable outcomes are those where despite some initial unpleasant event you are able to continue to enjoy life, e.g. surviving an aircraft crash unharmed or a company being able to stay in business
Non-recoverable outcomes	Dying in an aircraft crash or due to an error in a medical procedure

and many years before a final decision about risk acceptability is reached. In what follows, attention is focused mainly on major, corporate type risk decision situations such as those governments may have to take.

Important differences between large and small decisions on risk include the existence of a difference between the conscience of an individual as a decision-maker and the public conscience of the corporate body as a decision-maker. The personal exposure of the corporate decision-maker to the risk may be of a very different nature to the risk to which an individual will be exposed. Table 80 summarises some of the differences in the parameters associated with individuals' risk decisions and corporate bodies' risk decisions.

Certain risks may be regarded as unavoidable — both for the individual and for the corporate body. These include natural disasters, terrorist attacks, wars and revolutions. An unavoidable risk has to be accepted as part of life but this does not mean that no action can be taken to

Table 79. *Examples of multiple characteristics*

Risk	Characteristics
Soldier	Accepts risks on a voluntary basis (when it is a volunteer army). The risks may be increased when the orders the soldier is given have been badly thought out, or as a result of equipment failures, lack of skill or training on the soldier's part
Miner	A miner accepts the risks of working in a mine on a voluntary basis, although he may be under economic pressure to accept such work. The miner has no control over the working risks that may be attributable to the failures of others to observe safety procedures or to the occurrence of geological faults
Sports person	Accepts the risk on a voluntary basis, but may not be aware that the activity may worsen some inherent weakness in their body. They may be killed by a failure of their equipment or, in a sport such as boxing, by an opponent
Medical treatments	The possible outcomes of the treatment are that the patient recovers (life expectancy increased), the patient fails to recover, the patient's condition is made worse (life expectancy reduced), or there is just some temporary relief of the patient's condition. This means the risk may also have the characteristics of recoverable or non-recoverable outcome

reduce the impact of such events. The essential features of unavoidable risks are set out in Table 81.

Concern about death is an illustration of another way in which the views of individuals and corporations may differ. Generally speaking, the death of one person is given very little attention by the media; as a result there is little, if any, co-ordinated reaction. However, as the number of people killed in an incident increases — for example, when 20 people are killed in a train crash, or an oil rig failure kills 150 people or an aircraft crashes with loss of all on board — the scale of media attention increases giving rise to expressions of public outrage and calls for action to prevent a recurrence. The change of view about the acceptability of risk that is associated with the number of people killed or harmed in an incident may be represented graphically as in Fig. 15. This shows a non-dimensional relationship with a critical

Table 80. Differences between the parameters involved in individual and major/corporate risk decisions

Decision size	Parameters involved
Individual risk decision (such as deciding how to make a 200 km journey)	Availability of alternatives. Need/demand. Acceptability of alternatives (this may include reliability, comfort, speed, timing of public transport services, availability of fast roads, availability of parking and personal preferences)
Major/corporate risk decision (such as deciding to build a large chemical plant or launching a project to develop a new aeroplane)	Availability of funding. Demand for new development (there may be many forms of demand to be considerd). Feasibility (relevant technology known, skills required available, manufacturing facilities required available). Likely return on investment. Life of project. Regulatory restrictions such as planning, environmental, and health and safety regulations

Table 81. Essential features of unavoidable risks

Example	Essential feature
Earthquakes Volacanic eruptions Floods Storms Landslides	Only to a limited extent predictable. May damage buildings and structures. May cause loss of life
Terrorist attacks and wars	To a large extent unpredictable. Some security precautions may limit incidence and impact
Variation of the heat output of the sun	Unpredictable but changes detectable. (Some action possible to amelioriate impact of changes)
Genetic diseases	At present there are many diseases of genetic origin for which no treatment is possible. (There may in the future be scientific developments that change this view)

point when the number of people killed in a particular incident is close to or exceeds 50.

Two British cases where the public perception of risk gave rise to demands for a change to the regulatory regime to reduce the risk were the *Piper Alpha* oil rig disaster which killed 165 people,[138] and the

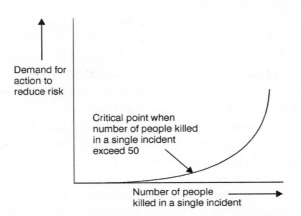

Fig. 15. Diagrammatic representation of the relationship between an event causing multiple deaths and the demand for action to be taken to reduce the risk involved

King's Cross underground station fire in which 31 people were killed.[139] In both cases there was a long official inquiry and as a result major changes were made to the health and safety regulatory system governing offshore oil and gas installations and the regulatory system for railways. Even accidents where nobody was killed — the fire in the Channel Tunnel mentioned in chapter 7 being such a case — can give rise to calls for increased precautions.

The risk of people being killed in war seems to fall into a different category. The public appears to be able to countenance the death of millions of people before a serious reaction occurs and this reaction is not always predictable. In the First World War, 8·5 million were killed and 21 million wounded. It is estimated that in the Second World War, 35 million died in the fighting and 10 million died in Nazi concentration camps.[140] Although in the First World War, Russia withdrew from the war because of the revolution in Russia, the war came to an end because there was a form of revolution in Germany. These revolutions were, at least in part, due to a reaction of the public to the number of casualties and the hardships that the war imposed. In contrast, even though the losses were higher, the Second World War was fought to the end by both sides. In the Second World War, Russia suffered many more millions of casualties than in the First World War, but there was no revolution as there had been in the First World War.

Another view of war is that some people consider there are moral issues or ways of life that are worth fighting for to the extent that young people are encouraged or forced to fight and to accept a higher than normal risk of being killed. The people who declare wars are not the people whose lives are at risk from being involved in fighting.

Perhaps all that can be said is that the acceptability of the risks of war is a special case somewhat removed from what we consider to be the risks of normal life. It may be that agreeing to participate in war is an example of a risk that is made acceptable by what are sometimes called *attitudinal certainties* — packages of beliefs that are reinforced by society to the extent that they become collective convictions.[141] Ordinary individuals are, to a large extent, conditioned or forced to accept the risks of war.

There is some experimental evidence to suggest that the public acceptability of a risk is influenced by the perceived frequency of the impact of the risk on the community involved.[142] For example, in a large community a particular risk with an associated probability of causing death would produce more deaths than if the same risk were applied to a smaller community. The research mentioned in reference 142 indicates that in a large community, because the risk is perceived as causing deaths more frequently than in a small community, people are more concerned about the risk than are people in a small community. This is, of course, the difference between perception and quantitative data and it is a factor that has to be considered in the determination of the acceptability of a particular risk.

All of the above constitutes an overall view of risk acceptability that suggests that the precise level of risk that is acceptable depends on the circumstances surrounding the risk and that in any situation there is a level of risk that marks the boundary of acceptability. It is possible that views on the level of risk acceptability may be biased because the population concerned bases its opinion on an incomplete understanding of the risk.

This section has tended to focus attention on the incidence of death as being the risk acceptability defining factor. This factor is, of course, not the only criterion for judging risk acceptability; there are many types of risk and many criteria for judging acceptability.

Common threads in risk acceptability

While there is no such thing as zero risk, people and organisations usually have some limit to the level of risk they are willing to accept. This limit is often unstated and among the general public rarely stated in precise quantitative terms. Nevertheless, it is the limit to risk acceptability that must be at the heart of any risk philosophy. Except for some special cases — such as the regulatory requirements for specific conditions — there are no universal national standards for the level of acceptable risk.[143] In many cases, the quantitative threshold of acceptable risk may not even be overtly discussed. In other cases, the threshold of acceptable risk may be variable and adjusted to circumstances or the magnitude of the risk. How, therefore, among this range of views of risk acceptability, may some common threads be found?

In the range of activities considered in earlier chapters it is possible to detect the existence of an at least implied limiting level of risk acceptability. In some cases, the risk was measured in fatalities, in others simply in terms of financial loss but identification of universal acceptability is complicated, in many cases, by the risk being influenced by the interaction of many more factors than just fatalities or financial loss. Systems analysis can help structure the identification of the associated factors, which in many ways represent the filaments from which a common thread can be spun.[144] In Fig. 16, some of the factors that make up the risk acceptability set are shown in a simplified form. Surrounding the risk acceptability set is the universal set which includes all the factors that make up life in general.

The figure shows only a representative sample of the most usual factors — those that are most likely to interact in a way that has some influence on the overall acceptability of a risk — but it shows sufficient to illustrate the character of the process. The fact that a factor may not be included in Fig. 16 does not imply that it cannot be important in some instances; in reality, while the factors that constitute the risk acceptability set will vary in detail from case to case, the essential nature of the pattern will not change.

The risk acceptability set identified in Fig. 16 is rather different to the set described earlier in Fig. 1 and the difference deserves some explanation if confusion is to be avoided. Fig. 1 represents a basic theoretical set and Fig. 16 represents the set in more general practical terms. There is a third form of the set, that is not described, that is the risk set for a specific case. Attention is drawn specifically to the inclusion, in Fig. 16, of individuals' and organisations' preferences which may be important factors in the risk acceptability set and may well have been conditioned by prior experience and beliefs.[145]

Acceptability is also influenced by the extent of communication and trust between the parties involved. Communication may, in some cases, be mainly in qualitative terms and some of the views expressed —

especially when the proposition being considered is novel — may be subjective opinions based on lack of knowledge of the subject.

For large decisions, the important aims of communication must be to determine the collective view of the acceptability of the proposition and to ensure that the parties involved have accurate information about the significance of the associated risk. The process of identifying the collective view will involve some weighting and integration of the opinions expressed; for example, the weight given to a convict's views on the efficacy of a new medical drug would differ from the weight given to the views of a specialist pharmacologist working in the field that includes the proposal. In practice, the weighting may be either an objective quantitative factor or an emotional subjective qualitative weighting based on the decision-maker's views of the importance of the factors involved. The possible variation in weighting is just one example of the influences that contribute to the degree of

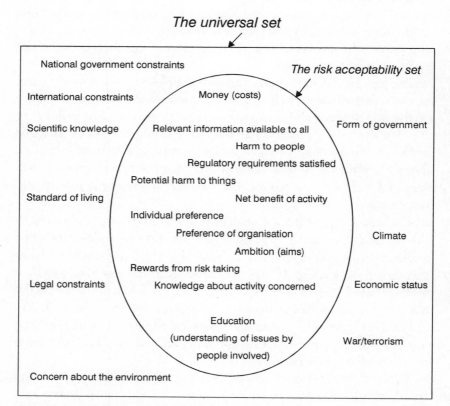

Fig. 16. A specific risk acceptability set

uncertainty associated with any evaluation of the acceptability of a risk.

In all cases, there is an element of trust between the suppliers of data about the nature of the options and the decision-maker. This bond of trust, if broken, can take a very long time to repair and until the bond is re-established decisions may be delayed or over-cautious decisions made. The issue of trust in decision-making has been explored by Slovic,[146, 147] who identified factors that appear to increase trust as well as those that would destroy trust. For trust in the validity of information about a large plant, some 46 factors were identified.

The question of trust is very closely related to knowledge and experience. There are many instances in life where people who are to make decisions about the acceptability of a risk do not have complete knowledge of all the risk implications of the proposition concerned. It may be something as simple as whether or not to allow a child to go out to play, or something more complicated such as whether or not all the properties of a new chemical are well enough understood to allow it to be marketed. In such situations the element of trust is clear, but in many other situations the element of trust may be much more obscure and its significance harder to identify. Some examples of situations where the role of trust may have wide implications are listed in Table 82. It could be argued that misplaced trust is simply an element of uncertainty that is likely to be present in all decision-making processes. Certainly, the

Table 82. Some situations where trust may have wide implications

Situation	Typical implications
Misleading information given on an application for insurance	Cover may not be valid or appropriate
Patient does not give doctor details of all his/her symptoms	Doctor may not be able to diagnose illness correctly
In a planning application a company may not identify all the materials it will be discharging to the environment	Application to build factory may be approved but the factory may become an environmental disaster
A company may ask a government to fund the development of a new military aeroplane. The funding asked for being less than the company knows the development will cost.	Development may take longer than expected due to delays caused by extra funding having to be obtained

better the knowledge of all the factors associated with a decision, the lower the element of trust required will be and the lower the uncertainty will be. The logical decision-maker will always make some allowance for uncertainty in the accuracy of the data on which decision-making has to be based.

A justifiable philosophy of risk acceptability

The conventional way of determining whether or not a philosophical proposition is justified is to test it, and then, from an analysis of the results, to assess its validity. The proposition under test in this instance is that there is, in most decision-making situations an identifiable level of risk acceptability and that this level of risk acceptability is related to the factors involved. The questions that must be answered are as follows.

- What is the test proposed?
- What are the likely results of the test?
- What conclusions are justified by the results of the test?

The range of factors that have to be considered in determining the acceptability of a risk are indicated in Fig. 16.

The specification proposed for the test is as follows.

- The risk to be considered is the acceptability of the uncertainty associated with building a chemical plant to make a new product within budget and to time.
- All the technical, economic and socio-political factors have been assessed in quantitative terms with the degree of uncertainty identified.
- Criteria for ranking or rating acceptability have been established, implying that an acceptable level of risk has been identified.

Table 83 shows how, for the test proposed, the factors identified in the risk acceptability set in Fig. 16 can be grouped under three all-embracing headings: technical; economic; socio-political.

It is assumed that under each of the three all-embracing factor headings is included the whole range of issues associated with that factor and that, taken together, every relevant issue is considered. For example, the technical factors include the following: all those aspects of the plant design required to construct a plant that will produce the product in the desired quantities and to the desired quality; the product's capability to perform in the way desired; all the environmental implications associated

Table 83. Relationship between the risk acceptability set and the test proposal data

Risk acceptability set factors	Test proposal data (all-embracing terms)	Characteristics
Harm to people Harm to things Knowledge of activity concerned Education Relevant information to satisfy regulatory requirements available	Technical	The activity to be assessed is understood precisely in technical and scientific terms
Money (costs) Rewards from risk taking (benefits) Net benefit of activity	Economic	The real benefits measured in terms of the through life difference between costs and benefits
Individual preference Preference of organisation Ambition (aims) Relevant information available to all	Socio-political	The aims of the proposal are acceptable to the public and the proposer

with the plant and all its outputs. Similarly, the economic factors include all the through life direct and indirect costs and benefits. (Considering the whole life implications of a proposal is an essential part of any decision-making process, as it is the only way of assessing the real impact of a proposition.) The socio-political factors include all the regulatory, legal, pressure group, political and public opinions that have to be considered in a democratic society.

With most issues, particularly when many people are involved, the question is whether there are some criteria for determining acceptability that are shared by all concerned. The owner of the plant will want the plant built, working and making money; if he/she has to seek finance, the institutions making the loan will want a return on their investment and the loan repaid. The socio-political factors are likely to have many foci which can generally be reduced to a single concept, namely, the plant has to be acceptable to the public. If the owner of the plant is a large company, its board will want to be convinced that the proposal is within the portfolio of risks the company is capable of accepting; if the owner has only a small business, the same issues will have to be considered but, having fewer resources, the owner will know that failure could have dramatic consequences and might ruin the company. It may be that the owner of a small business is a gambler and is willing to risk losing everything if the project fails; it may also be that the owner of the business, whether large or small, is very cautious and will check and recheck every aspect of the project in order to be convinced that the risk of failure is acceptably small. Whatever the size of the business, the owner may be willing to define the greatest acceptable overall probability of failure as 1 in 10^{-3} per year. (The choice of 1 in 10^{-3} being an acceptable probability for a risk does need some justification. We admit that to a large extent it is an arbitrary choice. We consider that in practical terms it is very difficult in many cases to prove errors are smaller than 1 in 10^{-3} or that something will not occur less frequently than 1 in 10^{-3}. A lot of very precise evidence is needed to show that the probability of an event occurring is less than 1 in 10^{-3}.) This limiting failure rate is intended to take into account all the possible forms of failure.

It is appreciated that acceptability may not be described in quantitative terms and that some other method of ranking acceptability — such as ordinal ranking or a letter coded system — may be used; some methods of ranking acceptability are summarised in Table 84.

It may be that the ranking or coding system adopted is specified as being directly related, in probability terms, to the risk specified. The advantage of the non-dimensional methods of ranking acceptability is that they overcome the problem of having to assess the significance of factors which have been described in different units; however, all the non-dimensional methods suffer from the shortcoming that they give

Table 84. Some methods of ranking acceptability

Method	Comment
In probability terms	Provided it is based on sound relevant information it is precise, but it needs to be supported by a statement of the risk involved
Ordinal ranking	Can be related to both frequency and type of risk
Letter coded ranking	Tend to be subjective unless exactly related to quantitative data
Acceptability defined in words	
Colour coded	

no clear indication of all the uncertainties that may be associated with a proposition. This lack of clarity about the associated uncertainties is a problem that may also be present when making an assessment in quantitative terms but it is a problem for which there are solutions.

The financier would be concerned that the risk of losing the money lent was small — perhaps also of the order of 1 in 10^{-3} per year — but in many commercial instances the loan would be covered by security on some asset of the proposer. (1 in 10^{-3} per year is not drawn out of the air, it is equal to the probability of death in a year of someone aged about 20. It is 1000 times greater than the risk of death due to being struck by lightning. It is higher than the risk of being killed in a road or flying accident. Put another way, gamblers participating in lotteries spend money on tickets when the chance of winning is much lower.) In economic terms, the overall assessment of the economic impact of a major project should include some assessment of the economic impact of the proposal on the national economy; this impact may be positive or negative when measured in terms of the excess of the through life value of benefits over costs incurred.

The probability that benefits will exceed costs will depend on the nature of the project; for example, the probability of benefits failing to exceed costs could be quite high (of the order of 10^{-2}) for an aid or charitable project while for a project with a product that is in high demand and which has a high commercial export value such a probability could be quite remote, say 10^{-4}. It must be recognised that products for which demand is high generally result in several suppliers entering the market, profit margins falling and changes in the balance of costs and benefits occurring over the life of the project in a way that may not have been predictable at the start. For very novel situations, or situations that involve making predictions about very uncertain future conditions, the increased risk may only be acceptable at a premium. It is apparent from this very brief examination that evaluations of risk may vary and that it is important to view the significance of limits from both sides.[148]

Perhaps the hardest factors to express in quantitative terms are the socio-political factors. However, if a survey of the opinions of people who might be in a position to support or oppose the project is carried out, it should be possible to arrive at a reliable estimate of the probability that the project will have the required level of socio-political support. Allowance should be made for the fact that this support may change with time; the probability of some kind of successful socio-political opposition to the project may be of the order of 1 in 10^{-2}.

The concept that these views of risk acceptability can be brought to a common measure was introduced in chapter 9 as was a methodology for so doing. Table 85 shows a possible way of assigning a comprehensive rating to risk acceptability; the figures given in the table are the overall risk figures for each factor.

In practice, building up the overall risk involves assessment of a myriad of components and factors. Something of the difference between component risk and overall risk can be illustrated by the risks associated with flying. Safety critical systems in civil transport aircraft require low failure probabilities of the order of one in 100 million flying hours but one third of accidents are typically attributed to engineering and general causes and two thirds are attributed to pilot error.[149] It has been suggested that pilots make potentially hazardous errors at rates in the range of 1 in 10 000 to 1 in 100 000 flying hours, but the flying career of a pilot is about 20 000 hours, so some pilots may never make a hazardous error. It has also been reported that although pilots have more than adequate individual capability, this is not being converted to the highest possible safety per flight. The suggestion has been made that the redundancy arrangements on the flight deck, based on two pilots and multiple systems, are not working as well as intended,[149] perhaps because the way

Table 85. Comprehensive rating of risk acceptability

Factor	Acceptable probability	Overall rating of acceptability	Comment
Technical	Acceptable risk of failure less than 10^{-3} in the life of the project		The overall acceptability is assessed in whole numbers. In the case considered the sum of the probabilities is $1 \cdot 2 \times 10^{-3}$ in the life of the project and that is taken as 1×10^{-3} in the life of the project which is just on the margin of acceptability
Economic	Acceptable risk of unacceptable economic benefit less than 10^{-4} in the life of the project	The overall integrated probability unacceptable factor should be equal to or less than 1×10^{-3} in the life of the project	
Socio-political	Acceptable risk of successful socio-political opposition to project less than 10^{-4} in the life of the project		

pilots cross-check each other's actions is not as effective in real flight as it is in studies performed in the simulator or in a laboratory. It could be that the lower performance is due to the stresses and distractions of real flight conditions being greater than those simulated in the laboratory but, whatever the cause, this digression into the risks associated with flying demonstrates that the more factors there are involved, the lower the risk has to be with each of them if a particular level of risk is to be achieved.

Returning to the example of the new chemical plant, were the detailed assessment of all the technical, economic and socio-political factors to show that the risk of unacceptable conditions arising at some stage in the project had a probability greater than 10^{-3}, it is likely that the project would be considered to be unacceptable. It must be stressed that any judgement about the acceptability of risk must be based on comprehensive assessment of **all** the factors involved; assessment simply based on individual risk criteria, cost/benefit analysis, societal risk (FN line criteria) and disutility (average harm) can give misleading results.

Any estimate of risk will, in real life, have some uncertainty associated with it; taking this into account would give upper and lower bounds to estimates of the probability of success. The upper and lower estimates may not be evenly distributed about the statistical mean and the distribution may be skewed resulting in the maximum frequency of occurrence (mode) of a risk being much higher — or lower — than the statistical mean or median.[150] The criterion adopted in the example that a risk probability of less than 1×10^{-3} is acceptable cannot be taken as a universal truth; the exact value will be determined by many factors including, importantly, whether the risk taker is a gambler or is over-cautious. As has been shown, other factors may also have an important influence on the level of acceptable risk; for example, in time of war it may be appropriate to accept higher risks than in peacetime and investment in building a commercial aircraft might require a much lower probability of failure. It is also important to recognise that the available data and the criteria for judging acceptability may change with time so that what might have been acceptable when a project was initially proposed may no longer be so several years on. Medical treatments considered acceptable in the 19th century may not be considered acceptable at the end of the 20th century and risks of car failure such as were experienced at the beginning of the 20th century will certainly be considered unacceptable at the end of the 20th century. Thus, the acceptability of the risks associated with a project must be kept under continual review throughout the life of the project.

Conclusions

If one takes an overall view of risk acceptability it is possible to detect that there is, in most decision-making situations, general acceptance of a particular level of risk. This acceptable level of risk is determined by the associated circumstances and influenced by the quality of the data available, the effectiveness of communication when explaining the significance of the risk, and the degree of trust that exists between all the parties involved. Each set of factors that makes up the environment surrounding the decision-making process has an influence on the level of the risk and its acceptability and, generally speaking, only risks whose probability is less than 10^{-3} are acceptable; any higher and action is required to reduce the level of risk. However, under exceptional circumstances, such as war or life saving operations, higher risks may be acceptable. These probabilities are very similar to the levels of risk acceptability criteria envisaged by the late Lord Ashby nearly 20 years ago.[151]

We would conclude that there is an identifiable level of acceptable risk for most activities and that if this level can be expressed in quantitative terms, it will assist those involved to make reliable decisions about the activity and the action required to deal with the risks. The more comprehensively a risk is understood, the more confidence there will be that a defensible decision can be made about its acceptability.

Finally, we suggest that underlying all decision-making is a philosophy that requires the risks associated with a proposition to be identified and to be shown to satisfy justifiable and consistent criteria of acceptability before the proposition itself can be considered to be acceptable. Unless the risks are identified and evaluated there can be no sound basis for making a decision about their acceptability — a simple philosophy that should be an essential part of every decision-maker's portfolio of guiding philosophies.

11

References

Chapter 1

1. KIRKWOOD A. Living with the public. *The Safety and Health Practitioner*, May, 1995.
2. *Risk and human behaviour*. Department of Economics of the University of Newcastle, 1997.
3. AYER A. J. *The central questions of philosophy*. Penguin Books Ltd., Harmondsworth, 1976, 1–2.
4. CHICKEN J. C. *Hazard control policy in Britain*. Pergamon Press, Oxford, 1975.
5. CHICKEN J. C. *Nuclear power hazard control policy*. Pergamon Press, Oxford, 1982.
6. CHICKEN J. C. *Managing risks and decisions in major projects*. Chapman and Hall, London, 1994.
7. CHICKEN J.C. Risk management: art or science? *Proc.12th Annual Conf. of the Major Projects Association*, London, 1994.
8. *Sigma*, No. 2/1996, Swiss Reinsurance Company, Zurich, Switzerland, 13.
9. *Sigma*, No. 2/1996, *op. cit.*, 39.
10. *Sigma*, No.2/1996, *op cit.*, 38.
11. HAYWARD D. Weather eye on revision. *New Civil Engineer*, 6 Feb., 1997, 26–27.
12. MERKHOFER M. W. *Decision science and social risk management*. D. Reidal Publishing Company, Boston, 1986, 187.
13. ASHBY E. *Reconciling man with the environment*. Oxford University Press, London, 1978, 38–9.

Chapter 2

14. WILLIAM B. Ethics. In Grayling A. C. (ed.), *Philosophy*. Oxford University Press, Oxford, 1995, 548–49.
15. SCHRADER-FRECHETTE K. S. *Science policy, ethics and economic methodology*. D. Readily Publishing Company, Dordrecht, Holland, 1984, preface and ch. 2.
16. POPPER K. R. *Objective knowledge – an evolutionary approach*. Oxford University Press, London, 1972, 32–3.
17. *Risk, its assessment, control and management*. The Chemical Industries Association, London, 1995.
18. RUSSELL B. *History of western philosophy*. Routledge, London, 1995, 788–89.
19. *Steven's Handbook of experimental psychology*. John Wiley and Sons, New York, 1988, 2nd edn, **2**, 722–23.
20. SLOVIC P. Perception of risk in decision-making. In Chicken J. C. (ed.), *Risk Handbook*. International Thomson Business Press, London, 1996, 24–9.

Chapter 3

21. *We innovate faster*. Steinbeis-Stiftung für Wirtschaftsförderung, Stuttgart, Germany, 1995.
22. DYER J. H. How Chrysler created an American Keiretsu. *Harvard Business Review*, July-Aug., 1996, 42–56.
23. *Good health is good business*. The Health and Safety Executive, London, 1995.
24. FOSTER P. Social worker wins £175 000 after stress ends career. *The Times*, 27 Apr., 1996, 6.
25. LGC Net (Local Government Chronicle Network) printout of information on council employee stress case background data.
26. TUC-IOSH-CBI. *Empowering safety professionals for better safety standards*. TUC consultative document, 1967.
27. The polluter pays? In *Health and Safety at Work*, 1994, 9.
28. ARTHUR W. B. Increasing returns and the New World business. Harvard Business Review, July-Aug., 1996, 100–09
29. CHECKLAND P. Soft systems methodology and an application of soft systems methodology. In Rosenhead J. (ed.), *Rational analysis for a problematic world*. John Wiley and Sons Ltd, Chichester, 1989, 71–120.
30. CHECKLAND P. *Systems thinking, systems practice*. John Wiley and Sons Ltd, Chichester, first published 1981 and reprinted 1984, 1985, 1986 and 1988.

Chapter 4

31. Insurance derivatives and securitization: new hedging perspectives for the US catastrophe insurance market. *Sigma*, No. 5/1996, Swiss Reinsurance Company, Zurich, Switzerland, 4.

32. Insurance derivatives and securitization: new hedging perspectives for the US catastrophe insurance market, *op. cit.*, 8.

33. GRAHAM G. Banks design new way of measuring credit exposure. *Financial Times*, London, 2 Apr., 1997, 16.

34. THORNHILL W. T. *Risk management for financial institution bankers.* Rolling Mills, Ill., 1990.

35. CLARK E. and MARIOS. *Managing risk in international business.* International Thomson Business Press, London, 1996.

36. BUTTICKER B. Implicit ratings of emerging markets. *Economic and Financial Prospects* No 6. /1996, Dec./Jan. Swiss Bank Corporation, Basle, Switzerland.

37. KEASEY K. and WATSON R. The state of art of small firm failure prediction: Achievements and Prognosis. *The International Small Business J.*, published by Woodcock Publications Ltd, Macclesfield, **9**, 4, 1991.

38. HODGSON G. J. Design and build — effects of contractor design on highway schemes. *Proc. Instn Civ. Engrs, Civ. Engng*, **108**, 2, May, 1995, 67.

39. THOMPSON P. and PERRY J. (eds), *Engineering construction risks.* Thomas Telford, London, 1992, 4.

40. CHICKEN J. C. Risk management: art or science? *Proc. 12th Annual Conf. of the Major Projects Association*, Oxford, Oct., 1994, 65. (Available from: Major Projects Association, Templeton College, Oxford.)

41. HSE report rips method apart. *New Civil Engineer*, 16 May 1996, 4–5.

42. ASCHINGER G. The nature of financial crises. *Economic and Financial Prospects* No. 3 /1996, July/Aug., Swiss Bank Corporation, Basle, Switzerland, 2–19.

43. BLUMLI W. D. Taking the surprise factor out of provisioning. *Economic and Financial Prospects* No. 1 /1997, Feb./Mar., Swiss Bank Corporation, Basle, Switzerland, 2–5.

44. Swiss Bank Corporation. *Annual Report 1996.* Swiss Bank Corporation, Basle, Switzerland, 46.

Chapter 5

45. CHICKEN J. C. *Managing risks and decisions in major projects.* Chapman & Hall, London, 1994.

46. OLIVER A. Ring of confidence. *New Civil Engineer*, 21/28 Dec., 1995, 10–11.

47. DONNE. M. *Leader of the Skies.* Frederick Muller Ltd., London, 1981, 84–113.

48. GAINS M. The risk business. *Aerospace*, **21**, 5, May, 1994, J. Royal Aeronautical Soc., London, 16–19.

49. MARCH P. R. *Brace by wire, fly by wire.* The Royal Airforce Benevolent Fund Enterprises, 1993, 146.

50. GARDNER C. *British Aircraft Corporation*. Book Club Associates, London, 1981, 119.

51. ROBINSON B. R. Aviation in Manchester: a short history. Manchester branch of the Royal Aeronautical Soc., 1977, 70 and 82–83.

52. *The Centenary Journal. The Royal Aeronautical Society 1866–1966.* **70**, 661, Jan., 1966, 97, 131, 137, 265.

53. BARNES C. H. *Bristol aircraft since 1910*. Third edn, Putman Aeronautical Books, London, 1988, 322–330.

54. FAUROUX R. The Government as an owner and participant. *Proc. 12th Annual Conf,* Oxford,. Oct., 1994, 3. (Available from: Major Projects, Association, Templeton College, Oxford.)

55. MARTIN T. and MACLEOD I. A. The Tay rail bridge disaster — a reappraisal based on modern analysis. *Proc. Instn Civ. Engrs*, **108**, 2, May, 1995, 77–83.

56. SALPUKAS A. Propelled toward disaster? *International Herald Tribune*, 29 Dec., 1995, 1.

57. McLARIN K. J. Thalidomide is back, but in a new role. *International Herald Tribune*, 29 Dec., 1 and 10.

58. COLBORN T., DUMANOSK D. and MYERS J. P. *Our stolen future*. Little, Brown and Company, London, 1997, 13–28, 158–59 and 240–49.

59. MORRIS P. W. G. *The management of projects*. Thomas Telford, London, 1994.

60. DBFO winners. CE Roads Supple. *New Civil Engineer*, 16 May, 1996, 29–32

61. Non-proportional reinsurance of losses due to natural disaster in 1995: Prices down despite insufficient cover. *Sigma*, No. 6/1995, Swiss Reinsurance Company, Economic Research Section, Zurich, Switzerland, 5.

62. *Risk and reward*. Private Finance Panel, May, 1996, 1.

63. LUEHRMAN T. A. What's it worth? *Harvard Business Review*, May/June, 1997, 132–42

64. LUEHRMAN T. A. Using APV: a better tool for valuing operations. *Harvard Business Review*, May/June 1997, 145–54

Chapter 6

65. Standardisation and validation of the use of pulmonary epithelial cells for toxicity assessment of occupational agents and drugs. *Biomedical and Health Research*, **7**, 1, Apr., 1996, 6.

66. *World Health Statistics, 1993*, World Health Organisation, Geneva, Switzerland, 1994.

67. DRISCOLL M. AND CONNER S. Crying shame of the vaccination victims. *The Sunday Times*, 3 Aug., 1997, 12.

68. Statistics of deaths reported to Coroners England and Wales 1995. Home Office Statistical Bulletin, 5/96, 8.

69. *The costs to the British economy of work accidents and work-related ill health.* Health and Safety Executive (HSE) Books, 19.

70. THOMPSON C. Dead reckoning. *Sunday Times Magazine*, 29 June, 1997, 14–21.

71. TOMIJANOVIC C. Book review. *Risk Analysis*, **16**, 6, New York, Dec., 1996, 849–50.

72. ILSI Risk Science Institute Pathogen Risk Assessment Working Group. A conceptual framework to assess the risk of human disease following exposure to pathogens. *Risk Analysis*, **16**, 6, New York, Dec., 1996, 841–48.

73. 75/318/EEC. Council Directive of the 20 May, 1975 on the approximation of the laws of Member States relating to analytical, pharmaco-toxicological and clinical standards and protocols in respect of the testing of proprietary medical products. European Economic Community, Brussels, 1975.

74. 83/571/EEC. Council recommendation of 26 Oct., 1983, concerning tests relating to the placing on the market of proprietary medicinal products. European Economic Community, Brussels, 1983.

75. Doctors say health care rationing is inevitable. *The Times*, 21 June, 1996, 9.

76. LAURANCE J. Operations and drugs could carry warning of risk. *The Times*, 26 Sep., 1996, 7.

77. A patent cure-all? *The Economist*, 15 June, 1996, 107.

78. BIOMED 2 – Outcome of first call. *Biomedical and Health Research*, **6**, 2, Nov., 1995, 4.

79. MILLER H. I. Responding to risk. In *Phizer Forum Europe*, 1997,

80. VAN DER DRIFT D. 'Watch for your skin' campaign finds widespread support among outdoor workers. *Janus*, 23, 1–1996, 3.

81. *On the state of the public health, 1995.* HMSO, London, 1996.

Chapter 7

82. THE DEPARTMENT OF TRANSPORT. *Transport Statistics Great Britain 1993*, HMSO, London, 1995, 170–181.

83. THE DEPARTMENT OF TRANSPORT. *Transport Statistics Great Britain 1993*, *op. cit.*, 162, 163 and 167.

84. FLEMING D. Calais linkspan failure forces system rethink. *New Civil Engineer*, 5 Sep. 1996, 5.

85. *Supplementary graphs and tables for road accident report*, 1994. Hertfordshire County Council, 1995.

86. BLACKMAN T. Safety requires a system not just regulation. *Aerospace*, J. Royal Aeronautical Society, **24**, 4, Apr., 1997, 16–21.

87. BATCHELOR C. Rights and wrongs of passage. *The Financial Times*, 24 Nov., 1996, 9.

88. THE DEPARTMENT OF TRANSPORT. *Transport Statistics Great Britain 1995*, *op. cit.*, table 5.31, 124.

89. THE DEPARTMENT OF TRANSPORT. *Transport Statistics Great Britain 1995*, *op. cit.*, table 1.1, 14.

90. *Railway safety*. Health and Safety Executive, London, 1992, table, appendix 4, 71.
91. THE DEPARTMENT OF TRANSPORT. *Transport Statistics Great Britain 1995*, op. cit., table 7.1, 153.
92. THE DEPARTMENT OF TRANSPORT. *Transport Statistics Great Britain 1995*, *op. cit.*, table 7.2, 155.
93. THE DEPARTMENT OF TRANSPORT. *Transport Statistics Great Britain 1995*, *op. cit.*, table 7.8, 163.
94. GIBSON H. Fear of flying over Africa. *Time*, 3 Feb., 1997, New York, 48–9.
95. THE DEPARTMENT OF TRANSPORT. *Transport Statistics Great Britain 1995*, *op. cit.*, table 7.8, 164.
96. THE DEPARTMENT OF TRANSPORT, *Transport Statistics Great Britain 1995*, *op cit.*, table 7.8, 165.
97. THE DEPARTMENT OF TRANSPORT. *Transport Statistics Great Britain 1995*, *op. cit.*, table 7.9, 166.
98. Air Transport. *Aerospace*, J. Royal Aeronautical Society, **23**, 4 Apr., 1996, 6.
99. PENNEY S. Some safety challenges. *Aerospace*, J. Royal Aeronautical Society, **24**, 2, Feb., 1997, 9–11.
100. SKAPINKER M. Old aircraft rise above doubts. *Financial Times*, 18/19 May, 1996, 3.
101. KINSLEY M. Less cost, more risk. *Time*, New York, 15 July, 1996, 57.
102. TOMKINS R. No fear of flying. *The Financial Times*, 20 June, 1996, 1.
103. Safety–some philosophy and some progress. *Aerospace*, J. Royal Aeronautical Society, **23**, 3, Mar., 1996, 13–15.
104. *Aerospace*, **22**, 1, Jan., 1995, J. Royal Aeronautical Society, 7.
105. TYE W. Civil airworthiness. *The Centenary Journal. The Royal Aeronautical Society 1866–1966*. **70**, 661, 253.
106. TYE W. Civil airworthiness. *op. cit.*, 254–55.
107. TYE W. Civil airworthiness. *op. cit.*, 256–57.
108. THE DEPARTMENT OF TRANSPORT, *Transport Statistics Great Britain 1995*, *op. cit.*, table 6.12, 14.
109. THE DEPARTMENT OF TRANSPORT, *Transport Statistics Great Britain 1995*, *op. cit.*, table 6.14, 143.
110. THE DEPARTMENT OF TRANSPORT, *Transport Statistics Great Britain 1995*, *op. cit.*, table 6.19, 148.
111. MOSES L. N. and SAVAGE I. Identify dangerous trucking firms. *Risk Analysis*, **16**, 3, June, 1996, New York, 359–66.
112. DUNN J. Forty tonnes of trouble. *Professional Engng*, Instn Mech. Engrs, **20** Nov., 1996, 15.
113. A bridge too far? editorial comment in *Professional Engng*, *op. cit.*, 3.
114. CHITTENDEN M., RAMESH R. and HAYNES S. What price safety? *Sunday Times*, 24 Nov., 1996, 17.
115. PATLOVANY R. W. US Aviation Regulations increase probability of mid air collisions. *Risk Analysis*, **17**, 2, Apr., 1997, New York, 237–48.

Chapter 8

116. NICHOLL J.P., COLEMAN P. and WILLIAMS B. T. A *national study of the epidemiology of exercise-related injury and illness*. The Sports Council, London, 1993.

117. Office of Population Censuses and Surveys. *General Household Survey 1987*. Social Survey Division, Series GHS No. 17, HMSO, London, 1989.

118. STUTTAFORD T. Why golfers are statistically more likely than the bone idle to suffer a heart attack. *The Times*, 15, June 1996, 9.

119. KISSEL J. C. RICHTER K. Y. and FENSKE R. A. Field measurement of dermal soil loading attributable to various activities: implications for exposure assessment. *Risk Analysis*, **16**, 1, New York, 1996, 115–25.

120. A winning history. *Connections*, Summer, 1996, BLA Group Ltd, London, 1996, 8.

121. KOGAN H. Sporting work. *Health and safety at work*, Oct., 1997, 10–12.

122. SLOVIC P. FISCHHOFF B. and LICHTENSTEIN S. Facts and fears: understanding perceived risk. In Schwing R. C. and Alhers W. A. (eds), *Societal Risk Assessment*, Plenum Press, New York, 1980, 181–216.

123. JAKUS P. M. and DOUGLAS SHAW W. An empirical analysis of rock climbers' response to hazard warnings. *Risk Analysis*, **16**, 4 Aug., 1996, New York, 581–86.

124. Sporting Injuries. The Sunday Times guide, *Change your Life*, prepared in association with PPP Healthcare, 11 Feb., 1996, 28–9.

Chapter 9

125. BEATTIE J. and LOOMES G. The impact of incentives in risky choice experiments. *The Economic Beliefs and Behaviour Programme*, Economic and Social Research Council, Swindon, May, 1996.

126. SOUZA PORTO M. F. and FREITAS C. M. Major chemical accidents in industrialising countries: the socio-political amplification of risk. *Risk Analysis*, **16**, 1, Feb., 1996, New York.

127. METZ W. C. Historical application of a social amplification of risk model: economic impacts of risk events at nuclear weapons facilities. *Risk Analysis*, **16**, 2, 1996, New York, 185–193.

128. SEILER F. A. and ALVAREZ J. L. On the selection of distributions for stochastic variables. *Risk Analysis*, **16**, 1, Feb., 1996, New York.

129. CHICKEN J. C. *Managing risks and decisions in major projects*. Chapman and Hall, London, 1994.

130. CHICKEN J. C. *Risk handbook*. International Thomson Business Press, London, 1996.

131. ARROW K. J. *Social choice and individual values*. Yale University Press, New Haven, 2 edn, 1963.

132. SHARMA S. *Applied multivariate techniques*. John Wiley & Sons Inc., New York, 1996.

133. PETERS, R. G. COVELLO V. T. and McCALLUM D. B. The determinants of trust and creditability in environmental risk communication: an empirical study. *Risk Analysis*, **17**, 1, Feb., 1997, New York, 43–54.

Chapter 10

134. LE POIDEVIN J. 'A partnership of effort' for reducing violence in schools. *Health, Safety and Environment Bulletin*, May, 1977, 14.
135. ASHBY E. *Reconciling man with the environment*. Oxford University Press, 1978, 73–87.
136. OTWAY H. J. and EDWARDS W. *Application of a simple multi-attribute rating technique to evaluation of nuclear waste disposal sites*. The International Institute for Applied Systems Analysis, Laxenberg, Vienna, 1977.
137. GORI G. B. Epidemiology, risk assessment, and public policy restoring epistemic warrants. *Risk Analysis*, **16**, 3, June, 1996, New York, 291–93.
138. Cm 1310. *The public inquiry into the Piper Alpha disaster*. HMSO, London, 1990.
139. Cm 499. *Investigation into the King's Cross underground fire*. HMSO, London, 1988.
140. GRUN B. *The timetables of history*. Simon and Schuster Inc., New York, 1991 edn, 473 and 524.
141. MARRIS C. and LANGFORD I. No cause for alarm. *Risk and Human Behaviour*, 1, March, 1997, Economic and Social Research Council, 7.
142. WEINSTEIN N. D., KOLB K. and GOLDSTEIN B. D. Using time intervals between expected events to communicate risk magnitudes. *Risk Analysis*, **16**, 3, New York, June, 1996, 305–08.
143. SUTER A. W. Response to 'Comment on an approach for balancing health and ecological risks at hazardous waste sites'. *Risk Analysis*, **16**, 3, New York, June, 1996, 299.
144. CHECKLAND P. *Systems thinking, systems practice*. John Wiley and Sons Ltd, Chichester, reprinted 1988.
145. BOLGER F. and HARVEY N. Psychological factors in risk taking behaviour. *Risk and Human Behaviour*, 2, 1997, Economic and Social Research Council, 5–7.
146. SLOVIC P. Perceived risk, trust and democracy. *Risk Analysis*, **13**, 6, 1993.
147. CHICKEN J. C. *Risk handbook*. International Thomson Business Press, London, 1996, 24–9.
148. AYER A. J. *Language, truth and logic*. Penguin Books, Harmondsworth, 1976, 47.
149. HOWARD R. Analysing pilot error. *Aerospace International*, **24**, 10, Oct., 1997, 28–30.
150. *Change in provisioning methodology*. Swiss Bank Corporation, Basle, Sep., 1996.
151. ASHBY E. *Reconciling man with the Environment*. Oxford University Press, 1978, 69–72.

Appendix 1
General data on losses

The data* in this appendix illustrate the magnitude of various types of loss and show what a high proportion of losses are due to natural catastrophes. In interpreting the data, allowance must be made for the regional nature of some losses.

Table 86 (below and overleaf). List of major losses in 1996 according to loss category

	No.	Group % of total	Victims including missing	Group % of total	Insured losses US$ million	Group % of total
NATURAL CATASTROPHES						
All natural catastrophes	129	37·8	31 950	62·8	7906·1	64·1
Floods	44		6853		233·1	
Storms	50		5385		5252·4	
Earthquake	8		544		0·0	
Drought, bush fires	7		97		0·0	
Cold, frost	10		779		2360·0	
Other	10		292		60·6	
MAN-MADE DISASTERS						
All man-made disasters	212	62·2	8267	37·2	4426·2	35·9
Major fires, explosions	37	10·9	595	2·7	2102·0	17·0
Industry, warehouses	20		54		1156·0	
Oil, gas	3		9		212·0	
Hotels	2		179		0·0	
Department stores	3		79		0·0	
Other buildings	9		274		734·0	
Other	0		0		0·0	

Table 86 — continued

	No.	Group % of total	Victims including missing	Group % of total	Insured losses US$ million	Group % of total
Aviation disasters	35	10·3	1976	8·9	813·7	6·6
Crashes	25		1658		301·1	
Explosions, fires	0		0		0·0	
Damage on ground	2		0		52·0	
Air collisions	2		312		36·0	
Space	7		6		424·6	
Other	0		0		0·0	
Shipping disasters	40	11·7	2822	12·7	194·3	1·6
Freighters	8		123		136·2	
Passenger ships	29		2673		0·0	
Tankers	2		26		32·4	
Drilling platforms	1		0		25·7	
Other	0		0		0·0	
Road/rail disasters	57	16·7	1526	6·9	373·2	3·0
Buses, trucks	31		975		0·0	
Rail	16		299		365·5	
Major pile-ups	1		11		0·0	
Other	9		241		7·7	
Mining accidents	5	1·5	265	1·2	0·0	0·0
Collapse of buildings/bridges	7	2·1	241	1·1	0·0	0·0
Miscellaneous	31	9·1	842	3·8	943·0	7·6
Terrorism, social unrest	19		468		893·5	
Other	12		374		49·5	
Total	*341*	*100·00*	*22 217*	*100*	*12 332·3*	*100*

* With the kind permission of Swiss Re the data in these tables are drawn from the publication *Sigma*, No. 3/1997.

Table 87. The 20 most costly insurance losses, 1996

Insured losses (in US$ millions)	No. of victims (dead and missing)	Event	Date	Country
1600	39	Hurricane *Fran*, wind speeds up to 193 km/hr	5.9–8.9	USA
735	59	Cold spell; including damage to Florida's citrus plantations	31.1–6.2	USA
659	0	Car bomb explosion in front of shopping centre	15.6	UK
600	32	Snowstorm paralyses road, rail and air traffic on east coast of USA	6.1–9.1	USA
585	120	Winter storm	12.1–13.1	USA
404	0	Head office of Credit Lyonnais gutted by fire	5.5	France
395	32	Snowstorms and freezing weather in the midwest; floods after thaw on east coast	17.1–20.1	USA
375	0	Wind, hail, tornadoes, floods	24.5–29.5	USA
366	0	Fire on goods train in Channel Tunnel damages 600 m length of northbound section	18.11–19.11	France/UK
315	16	Major fire in Dusseldorf airport following welding work; toxic fumes released	11.4–12.4	Germany
305	6	Series of 65 tornadoes and storms in the midwest; insured damage in Arkansas alone US$ 250 million	19.4–22.4	USA
300	0	Storms, hail, floods	3.5–11.5	USA
266	0	Explosion in semiconductor plant	14.1	Taiwan
240	6	Bad weather front on the tail of hurricane *Lili* hits western Europe	27.10–30.10	Europe
230	2	Bomb attack in Docklands in London	9.2	UK
218	6	Chinese carrier rocket 'Long March 3B' with US Intelsat–708 on board explodes immediately after launch	16.2	China
210	0	Storms, hail, floods	16.3–21.3	USA
194	27	Hurricane *Bertha*, wind speeds up to 185 km/hr	9.7–14.7	USA
175	6	Explosion in petrochemical plant due to faulty maintenance work	26.7	Mexico
170	0	Wind, floods	18.10–21.10	USA

Table 88 (below and facing). The 20 worst catastrophes in 1996 involving fatalities

No. of Victims (dead and missing)	Insured damage (in US$ millions)	Event	Date	Country
2000	0	Cyclone and rainfalls over southeast coast; harvest destroyed	6.11–7.11	India
1500	0	Monsoon, worst floods for at least 50 years; 98 000 houses destroyed	30.6–26.7	China
1200	0	High-water overflow in three rivers after non-stop rain	1.8–14.8	China
869	0	Ferry *Bukoba* sinks on Lake Victoria	21.5	Tanzania
600	0	Tornado in the north of the country destroys approx. 80 villages	13.5	Bangladesh
500	0	Floods submerge approx. 2·96 million hectares of land; harvest and livestock lost	25.8–1.9	India
350	0	Antonov AN–32 cargo plane crashes on to busy market place shortly after take-off	8.1	Zaire
446	0	Heavy rains cause severe flooding in central Yemen	13.6–2.7	Arab. Rep. of Yemen
338	0	Floods following rain; several reservoirs burst; damage to crops	16.10–24.10	India
312	36	Saudi Airlines Boeing 747 collides with a Kazakh Airlines Tupolev Tu–154 cargo plane at 6500m	12.11	India
304	0	Earthquake (Richter scale 7) destroys 340 000 timber houses	3.2	China
284	0	Rain, floods, landslides; harvest loss in a country battling with food shortages since 1995	26.7–28.7	North Korea
244	0	Landslides in the northeast following monsoon; houses buried in the village of Jhagraku	5.8	Nepal
229	11	TWA Boeing 747–131 explodes and crashes into sea shortly after take-off	17.7	USA
226	0	Pilgrims surprised by sudden cold spell; snow, rain and landslides	23.8–25.8	India

Table 88 — continued

No. of Victims (dead and missing)	Insured damage (in US$ millions)	Event	Date	Country
220	0	Ship sinks off the southeast coast	24.1	Nigeria
200	0	Freezing weather from Spain to Siberia; avalanches, snowstorms, sleet	27.12–5.1	Europe
194	0	Tornado; storms and floods in the Red River Delta, landslides	14.8–26.8	Vietnam
190	0	Monsoon rain, floods and landslides	22.6–18.7	India
189	34	Birgenair Boeing B–757 crashes into the Atlantic Ocean	6.2	Dominican Rep.

Table 89 (below and overleaf). The 40 most costly insurance losses, 1970–1996

Losses in US$ millions at 1996 prices	Fatalities (including dead and missing)	Date/start	Event	Country
17 945	38	24.8.92	Hurricane *Andrew*	USA
13 277	60	17.1.94	Northridge earthquake in southern California	USA
6420	51	27.9.91	Tornado *Mireille*	Japan
5531	95	25.1.90	Winter storm *Daria* (severe gales)	Europe
5326	61	15.9.89	Hurricane *Hugo*	Puerto Rico
4151	13	15.10.87	Autumn storm	Europe
3844	64	26.2.90	Winter storm *Vivian*	Europe
2662	167	6.7.88	Explosion on offshore platform *Piper Alpha*	UK

Table 89 — continued

Losses in US$ millions at 1996 prices	Fatalities (including dead and missing)	Date/start	Event	Country
2554	6000	17.1.95	Great Hanshin earthquake in Kobe	Japan
2170	59	4.10.95	Hurricane *Opal*	USA
1906	246	10.3.93	Blizzard over east coast	USA
1795	4	11.9.92	Hurricane *Iniki*	USA
1682	23	23.10.89	Explosion at Phillips Petroleum	USA
1629	0	3.9.79	Tornado *Frederic*	USA
1600	39	5.9.96	Hurricane *Fran* in the southeast	USA
1595	2000	18.9.74	Tropical cyclone *Fifi*	Honduras
1481	350	12.9.88	Tropical cyclone *Gilbert*	Jamaica
1389	500	17.12.83	Snowstorms, frost	USA
1386	26	20.10.91	Forest fire which spread to urban area, drought	USA
1373	350	2.4.74	Tornadoes in 14 US states	USA
1314	31	4.8.70	Tornado *Celia*	USA
1310	0	25.4.73	Flooding caused by Mississippi	USA
1270	63	17.10.89	Loma Prieta earthquake	USA
1173	21	5.5.95	Wind, hail and floods	USA
1127	100	2.1.76	Storms over northwestern Europe	Europe
1065	20	17.8.83	Hurricane *Alicia*	USA

Table 89 — continued

Losses in US$ millions at 1996 prices	Fatalities (including dead and missing)	Date/start	Event	Country
1035	3	26.10.93	Forest fire which spread to urban area	USA
1033	40	21.1.95	Storms and floods in northern Europe	Europe
1003	28	3.2.90	Storm *Herta*	Europe
976	47	3.9.93	Typhoon *Yancy*	Japan
970	13	18.8.91	Hurricane *Bob*	USA
954	36	16.2.80	Floods in CA and AZ	USA
953	0	28.3.79	Malfunction in Three Mile Island power station	USA
947	0	30.4.83	Storm and floods	France
919	15	28.2.90	Winter storm *Wiebke*	Europe
904	108	14.9.95	Hurricane *Marilyn*	Caribbean, USA
885	11	28.12.89	Earthquake in Newcastle	Australia
869	58	29.4.92	Race riots in Los Angeles	USA
852	0	28.4.92	Storm, hail, tornadoes in OK and TX	USA
850	0	17.1.94	Freezing weather and snowstorms hit east coast	USA

Table 90 (below and facing). The 40 worst catastrophes in terms of fatalities, 1970–1996

Fatalities (includes dead and missing)	Insured losses in US$ millions at 1996 prices	Date/start	Event	Country
300 000	0	14.11.70	Tropical cyclone	Bangladesh
250 000	0	28.7.76	Earthquake in Tangshan	China
140 000	0	29.4.91	Tropical cyclone *Gorky*	Bangladesh
60 000	0	31.5.70	Earthquake	Peru
50 000	139	21.6.90	Earthquake	Iran
25 000	0	7.12.88	Earthquake in Armenia	Former Soviet Union
25 000	0	16.9.78	Earthquake	Iran
23 000	0	13.11.85	Volcanic eruption *Nevado del Ruiz*	Columbia
22 000	207	4.2.76	Earthquake	Guatemala
15 000	471	19.9.85	Earthquake	Mexico
15 000	0	11.8.79	Damburst	India
15 000	0	1.9.78	Flood	India
10 800	0	31.10.71	Flood	India
10 000	0	25.5.85	Tropical cyclone	Bangladesh
10 000	0	20.11.77	Tropical cyclone	India
9500	0	30.9.93	Earthquake in the state of Maharashtra	India
8000	0	16.8.76	Earthquake in Mindanao	Philippines
6304	0	5.11.91	Typhoons *Thelma* and *Uring*	Philippines
6000	2554	17.1.95	Great Hanshin earthquake in Kobe	Japan
5300	0	28.12.74	Earthquake	Pakistan
5000	0	10.4.72	Earthquake in Fars	Iran
5000	378	23.12.72	Earthquake in Managua	Nicaragua
5000	0	30.6.76	Earthquake	Indonesia
4800	0	23.11.80	Earthquake	Italy
4500	0	10.10.80	Earthquake	Algeria

Table 90 — continued

Fatalities (includes dead and missing)	Insured losses in US$ millions at 1996 prices	Date/start	Event	Country
4000	0	15.2.72	Storm and snow	Iran
4000	0	24.11.76	Earthquake in Van	Turkey
3800	0	8.9.92	Floods in Punjab	Pakistan
3200	0	16.4.78	Tornado	Reunion
3000	0	1.8.88	Flood	Bangladesh
3000	0	11.6.81	Earthquake	Iran
3000	0	2.12.84	Malfunction in Bhopal chemical plant	India
2800	0	13.12.82	Earthquake in the north of the country	Arab Rep. of Yemen
2500	0	31.7.74	Floods in northern provinces	Bangladesh
2500	0	6.6.81	Railway accident in Bihar	India
2484	0	11.12.92	Earthquake in Flores Island	Indonesia
2300	0	29.11.88	Tropical cyclone	Bangladesh, India
2300	0	6.9.75	Earthquake (Richter scale 6.8)	Turkey
2000	0	6.11.96	Tropical cyclone over southeast coast	India
2000	1595	18.9.74	Tropical cyclone *Fifi*	Honduras

Appendix 2

Some major project disasters

The following list of major project disasters is simply intended to illustrate the nature of major project disasters in the civil engineering field, and not to be a comprehensive list of disasters.

- In 1996, a deck fracture occurred on the Palau Bridge. The bridge was the world's longest post-tensioned balanced cantilever bridge. The likely cause of the accident was that the bridge was overstressed during strengthening work.

- In 1974, while the Kempton bridge was being built in Germany, the centre span collapsed as concrete was being poured. Nine people were killed. The cause of the accident was failure of A-frame falsework supports.

- In 1980, at the bridge at Almo in Sweden, a ship hit an unprotected twin tube pier causing the bridge to collapse and the deck to fall into the fjord.

- In 1988, after a gas explosion on the *Piper Alpha* oil rig, a major fire occurred killing 165 people and incurring losses of £2 billion. It was the world's worst oil rig fire.

- In 1976, the German Seiton Canal was breached six months after filling owing to differential settlement caused by joint failure in the canal's asphaltic concrete membrane.

- In 1984, at Abbeystead, methane accumulation caused an explosion in an underground water transfer valve house. Sixteen people were killed. The cause of the accident was poor design of the gas venting pipe.

- In 1994, a tunnel being built for the Heathrow Express collapsed. The cause of the accident was inadequate control and management of the work.

Appendix 3

Risk assessment of medical procedures

The usual methods of risk assessment can be applied to medical procedures.* Like all assessments the accuracy of the assessment depends on the quality of the data available, and in the medical field good clinical or epidemiological data may not always exist. We do not want to give the impression that every general practitioner will carry out a quantitative risk assessment before signing a prescription. But we believe the philosophy of risk assessment will help guide the decision about the optional treatment for a patient.

Figure 17 shows a simplified fault tree of the degree of risk associated with the various treatment options available for a particular patient. The diagram shows that if appropriate tests are carried out successfully, the condition is correctly diagnosed and the most efficacious treatment given there is a 95% chance that the patient will survive. However, if no tests are made and the patient's condition is judged simply from external symptoms the chance of survival is lower. The reason being that the chance of being given the correct treatment is lower. In the case shown in the figure it was assumed that the chance of being given the correct treatment was 0·4. The estimate of the chance of survival can be refined as more data is available about the patient and the efficacy of the possible treatments. The additional data about the efficacy of treatments might show the characteristics as shown in Fig. 18.

Although the treatments shown are only hypothetical the diagram shows that some treatments may yield a higher initial survival rate and a lower long-term survival rate than other treatments. In the real world other factors would have to be considered like natural life expectancy, patient's general condition, costs and benefits and the availability of funds. The patient might have a different

* The arguments presented in this appendix have drawn heavily on the work of Professor Milton C. Weinstein and presented in his paper 'Risky choices in medical decision-making: a survey', published in *The Geneva Papers on Risk and Insurance*, **11**, 40, July, 1986, published by The Geneva Association, Geneva, Switzerland.

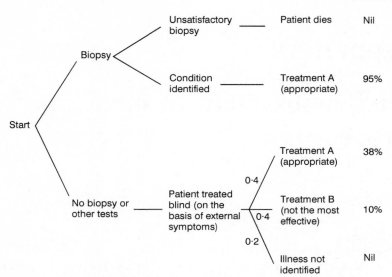

Fig. 17. *Fault tree for assessing the efficacy of various treatment options*

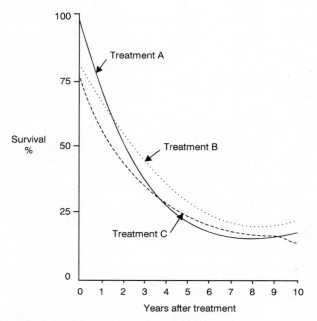

Fig. 18. *The efficacy of hypothetical treatments*

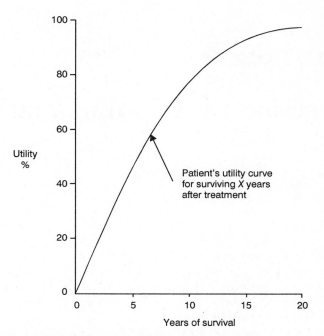

Fig. 19. A patient's utility curve for surviving treatment

view of the utility of surviving a particular number of years. The characteristic of the patient's utility care might take the form shown in Fig. 19. The arguments presented may be extended to cover the justification of the level of expenditure on health care.

Appendix 4

A version of the Hippocratic Oath

I will look upon him who shall have taught me this Art even as one of my parents. I will share my substance with him, and I will supply his necessities, if he be in need. I will regard his offspring even as my own brethren, and I will teach them this Art, if they would learn it, without fee or covenant. I will impart this Art by precept, by lecture and by every mode of teaching, not only to my own sons, but to the sons of him who taught me, and to disciples bound by covenant and oath, according to the Law of Medicine.

The regimen I adopt shall be for the benefit of my patients according to my ability and judgement, and not for their hurt or for any wrong. I will give no deadly drug to any, though it be asked of me, nor will I counsel such, and especially I will not aid a woman to procure abortion. Whatsoever house I enter, there will I go for the benefit of the sick, refraining from all wrongdoing or corruption, and especially from any act of seduction, of male or female, of bond or free. Whatsoever things I see or hear concerning the life of men, in my attendance on the sick, or even apart therefrom, which ought not to be noised abroad, I will keep silence thereon, counting such things to be as sacred secrets.

Appendix 5

Some important dates in the development of transport

1804	Richard Trevithick	First steam locomotive
1825	George Stephenson	First public railway Stockton–Darlington
1830	Liverpool–Manchester	First steam passenger line
1830	USA	First American built locomotive enters service in South Carolina
1853	Elisha Otis (USA)	First passenger lift
1859	Etienne Lenoir (France)	Internal combustion engine
1863	London	First underground railway
1869	George Westinghouse (USA)	Compressed air brake
1876	Graham Bell (Scotland)	First telephone
1879	Werner Von Siemens (Germany)	First electric train demonstrated in Germany
1885	Gottlieb Daimler & Karl Benz (Germany)	First petrol engine
1886	Gottlieb Daimler & Karl Benz (Germany)	First petrol engined four wheel vehicle
1890	London	First electric underground train
1900	Zeppelin (Germany)	First Zeppelin
1901	Wuppertal Schwebebahn (Germany)	World's first successful monorail enters service
1903	Wilber and Orville Wright (USA)	First powered flight
1911	Cadillac (USA)	Introduction electric starter and dynamo lighting
1912	Germany	First diesel locomotive
1920	Deusenberg (Germany)	Four wheel hydraulic brakes
1922	Lancia (Italy)	Monocoque construction and independent front suspension for motor cars

1926	Britain	Mallard sets steam speed record (125mph)
1928	Cadillac (USA)	Synchromesh gearbox
1930	Frank Whittle (Britain)	Jet engine invented
1934	Citroen (France)	Front wheel drive
1935	Carlton Magee (USA)	Parking meter
1938	Germany	First VW produced
1941	Swiss Federal Railways	Introduction gas turbine locomotive
1948	Michelin (France)	Introduction radial ply tyre
1948	Goodrich (USA)	Tubeless tyre
1950	Dunlop (Britain)	First disc brake
1951	Buick & Chrysler (USA)	Power steering
1952	DH Comet airliner (Britain)	First jet engined airliner to enter service
1954	BOSCH (Germany)	Fuel injection for cars
1955	Citroen (France)	Innovative body shape and hydropneumatic suspension
1955	Christopher Cockerall (Britain)	Hovercraft
1957	Felix Wankel (Germany)	Rotary engine
1957	Boeing and Douglas (USA)	Large jet powered airliners enter service
1959	Alex Isigonis (Britain)	BMC Mini
1964	Japan	210kph (130mph) Bullet train Osaka–Tokyo
1966	California	Legislation to reduce air pollution from cars
1970	Boeing (USA)	Jumbo jet enters service
1972	Dunlop (Britain)	Safety tyre (self sealing)
1973	Britain	HST diesel train achieves 229kph (143mph)
1976	Concorde Airline (Britain/France)	Supersonic airliner enters service
1979	Japan National Railways	Attains 517kph (321mph) with test vehicle
1981	France	TGV Paris–Lyon regularly reaches 270kph
1987	Japan	MAGLEV levitation train achieves 401kph
1990	France	TGV–OSE records 515kph (320mph) TGV Paris–Lyon averages 213 kph peaking at 299 kph
1994	Britain/France	Eurotunnel opens (connecting Britain and France)
1995	Britain	Eurostar enters full service (train between Britain and France using Eurotunnel)

Glossary

Adjusted Present Value (APV)	Is the value of a project as if it were financed entirely by equity, plus the value of all financing side effects such as tax, cost of financial distress and banking costs.
Bayesian techniques	A statistical method for iteratively refining subjective estimates as more objective data becomes available.
Biopsy	Examination of tissue removed from a living body.
Cost overruns	Claims that a contractor makes for payments to cover costs that were not allowed for in the original contract price.
Cost/benefit principles (as the term is used in chapter 2)	Trade-off between optimisation and simplicity in choosing the way to process information. (Making the most effective use of a particular situation.)
Deduction	Inferring from particular instances that a general law is true.
Discounted cash flow	The value of a particular investment to a business of future cash flows discounted to present value.
Equity Cash Flow (ECF)	Represents the expected cash flows to equity discounted at a discount rate that compensates for the risk being borne.
Experiment	Any process that generates a set of data.
FN-curve	A way of showing graphically the relationship between the tolerable

	probability and the number of fatalities expected from a particular type of accident.
Game theory	A methodology for assessing the implications of various strategies.
Gross Domestic Product (GDP)	The total value of goods and services produced within national boundaries and excludes income from abroad. Gross National Product (GNP) = GDP + net income from abroad.
Hard data or evidence	Data or evidence that can be expressed in precise quantitative terms with only a small degree of uncertainty.
Heuristic	Allowing a solution to be developed by trial and error.
Hippocratic Oath	An oath stating the obligations and proper conduct of physicians. The work of Hippocrates (*circa* 460–357 BC) has exerted considerable influence on medical ethics.
Holistic	Treating the whole problem or issue.
Indicative judgements	Judgements based on qualitative or speculative data.
Induction	Inferring from a general law that a particular case is true.
Knowledge	The sum of what is known either theoretically or practically.
Logit analysis	A relationship between cause and effect that is log log – that is the graph of the relationship between the two variables is sigmoidal in shape (shaped like an S) but it approaches the extremes (0% and 100%) more gradually than the probit model.
Media	Television, radio and press.
Multivariate analysis	Construction of a series of equations that together describe how the factors of interest behave under various circumstances.
Objective evidence	Evidence based on hard quantitative data.
Pathogen	Any disease-producing micro-organism or substance.
Perceptual processes	Selection of decision rules is done in a non-deliberative manner (selection procedures not carefully thought out and justified).
Probability	Is the likelihood of an event in a statistical

	experiment. The probability is defined in real numbers ranging from 0 to 1.
Probit analysis	A relationship between cause and effect that is log-normal – that is the graph of the relationship between the two variables is sigmoidal in shape but it approaches the extremes (0% and 100%) faster than the logit model.
Production systems	A system of comparing pairs of values of attributes to determine which alternative is the better.
Proposer	Body sponsoring a project.
Proximate decision-maker	A close adviser to the decision-maker.
Public inquiry	A British practice which involves a Government Minister appointing a leading figure, generally with a legal background, to conduct an inquiry into a controversial subject in order to advise him/her on the most appropriate course of action.
Qualitative data	Data based on opinion expressed in non-quantitative terms.
Quantitative data	Numerically expressed data based on observation, measurement or calculation.
Ranking	Ordering the significance of decision options and the sub-factors that have to be considered.
Ranking scales	An ordinal measure of the acceptability of a particular option or sub-factor.
Regulatory body	Body that has legal authority to set requirements that projects should satisfy and power to ensure that the requirements are satisfied.
Risk	The probability of an undesired outcome. In economic arguments it can mean an undesired outcome expressed in monetary terms.
Ro-Ro ferry	A ferry for transporting vehicles which are driven on or off.
Scholasticism	A form of arguing without a serious problem.
Soft data or evidence	Data or evidence that can only be expressed in qualitative terms that have a very large degree of uncertainty or variability associated with them.

Subjective evidence Evidence that is based on soft qualitative data.

Supersonic Faster than the speed of sound.

Teratogenic effects Causing malformation of an embryo.

Total risk The sum of the direct and indirect risks.

Transparency Transparency is when financial reports make the real financial position clear. Opaque or non transparency is when accounts obscure the real financial position of an organisation.

Trivial philosophy A philosophy that is limited in the range of factors considered.

Uncertainty Doubt about which there is no indication of the associated probability distribution.

Volatility The variation year to year in a company's financial performance. Sometimes the volatility can be judged on the variation in performance within a year, e.g. for a company whose trade is seasonal.

Weighting A constant by which a factor is multiplied in order to adjust the significance of the factor into its correct relationship with other factors.

Index